praise for

IT
STARTS
WITH
me

"*It Starts with Me* is an emotionally resonant, powerful, and hopeful story that will stay with me for a long time. If you are looking to be inspired, validated, understood, and seen; if you are in the process of your own great 'unbecoming'; if you are a mother wanting to create the best future for your children—pick up this book. Carmin Caterina is a luminous butterfly, and she will help you recognize your own inner monarch too!"

Dallas Woodburn, award-winning author of *Your Book Matters*

"*It Starts with Me: One Mom's Journey to End Generational Trauma* offers a compelling narrative that delves into the complexities of overcoming familial wounds. The author's storytelling is raw and evocative, providing an intimate look into the impact of trauma on decision-making. Through tales of love, loss, and resilience, the book navigates intergenerational patterns with a call to break free from cyclical behaviors. It guides those seeking healing, self-discovery, and a transformative journey toward a brighter future."

Chris Palmore, bestselling author of *The Mechanics of Gratitude*

"I am a better person for reading *It Starts with Me*. Carmin is unflinching in telling her raw, real truth, and in doing so, she creates an opportunity for us all. If you've ever been traumatized by life and are looking for real solutions from someone who has succeeded at healing those wounds, this book is for you!"

Kris Whitehead, #1 bestselling author and founder of Iconic Alliance

"This book contains life-changing information. Carmin Caterina tells a powerful story that is inspiring and transforming. *It Starts with Me* is great for anyone looking to better themselves and work through any past traumas. Bravo to Carmin for telling a beautiful story of hope and healing."

Christina Lombardi, RD, FMNS, author and registered dietitian

"How can a narrative recounting a woman's journey through trauma exude such abundant hope, synchronicity, and gratitude—yet refrain from casting blame? I deeply admire Carmin's ability to articulate her experiences, serving as a clarion call proclaiming, 'This is not okay,' for those who need to hear it. She has documented her own voice in a way that will serve as a support for so many who walk in those shoes. While reading, I am in tears, reassured. I hear Carmin saying, 'You are okay. Your voice is heard. Your experiences are valid. And your feelings are normal.'

This book transforms into both a testament, affirming that over-coming is possible for everyone, and a guidebook, illuminating the path to help. In honoring one woman's healing journey, the collective consciousness is stirred. Carmin pens this narrative not just for herself, but for all of us, our daughters, and our shared humanity. It echoes the sentiment that we should recognize our inherent resilience even on the days when love feels distant. In moments of uncertainty, the book becomes a beacon, reminding us that there is a way out, and our intuition is a steadfast guide, ever nudging us toward our own healing."

Gina LaVerde, medical intuitive

"*It Starts with Me*: a straight-from-the-heart, deep-in-your-soul look into the trials and tribulations of life choices, both good and bad. From the unbeknownst stages of the chrysalis to the full spreading of her wings, Carmin Caterina shows us all exactly how she dealt with the cyclical changes that we all face through the face of time. A must read!"

Jesse Inserra, author of *The Last Leaf*

IT
STARTS
WITH
me

One Mom's Journey
to End the Pattern of
Generational Trauma

carmin caterina

Published by

**MANDALA
TREE** PRESS
mandalatreepress.com

Paperback ISBN: 9781954801868
Hardcover with Dust Jacket ISBN: 9781954801882
Case Laminate Hardcover ISBN: 9781954801875
eBook ISBN: 9781954801899

FAM034000 FAMILY & RELATIONSHIPS / Parenting / General
SEL031000   SELF-HELP / Personal Growth / General
HEA055000 HEALTH & FITNESS / Mental Health

Cover design and typesetting by Kaitlin Barwick
Edited by Justin Greer and Melissa Miller

carmincaterina.com

For my daughters—my super generation.
Thank you for giving me purpose and a reason to heal.
May you fly faster and farther than you have
ever dreamed. I love you infinitely.

And for my Nonna, whose love saved my life.
Mi manchi tanto.

And to anyone who has ever been hurt by those people
entrusted with their care. May you know how much
you are deeply deserving of love, now and always.

Contents

Contents

Contents

Contents

No one would call what I did epic,
except maybe me.
I turned a life not worth living,
into a wanting to be alive for it.

Stacie Martin

Introduction

Butterfly Magic

The journey of the North American monarch butterfly is one of the most incredible natural phenomena in the world.

The monarch is the only butterfly species known to make a round trip migration in the fascinating way birds do. In fact, monarchs possess the most highly evolved migration pattern of any other butterfly species. Relying on an internal time clock and inner compass not entirely understood (as it cannot actually be seen), the monarchs instinctively know when and in what direction to travel.

Every summer, several generations of monarch butterflies are born, gradually making their way north. Although they have a life expectancy of only two to six weeks, before they die, they make sure to pass the baton to the next generation of butterflies to complete a journey that they themselves will never see. Believe it or not, it takes about four to five generations to complete the one-way voyage!

Along the way, these butterflies fly, mate, lay eggs, and eventually give birth to a new generation—but not without first undergoing an incredible transformation. Monarch

1

butterflies begin as tiny eggs on a milkweed plant. They then hatch into larvae (otherwise known as caterpillars). Next, they attach themselves to a perfect stem or leaf and spin silk, creating a pad-like structure that eventually becomes the pupa or chrysalis. Last, the old body parts of the caterpillar break down completely into a goo-like substance and change form entirely! The butterfly wings and organs then develop from cells that were already present in the larvae. This is absolutely unbelievable: the old version is vital to the creation of the new!

Unlike other butterflies, monarchs cannot survive the cold winters of the north. Come fall, the newest generation embarks on an even more incredible journey south, covering all the distance their ancestors traveled. But these butterflies are vastly different from any that came before them. These are a *Super Generation* of monarch butterflies, who will live much longer (up to eight months) and fly faster (possessing wings bigger than any previous generation), and travel much farther (sometimes up to 100 miles a day, totaling approximately 2,800 miles) than their parents, grandparents, great-grandparents, and sometimes great-great-grandparents ever have!

These millions of tiny orange compasses with wings eventually find themselves 10,000 feet above sea level, making their winter home atop the oyamel trees in the Sierra Madre Mountains in Mexico! Tens of thousands of butterflies inhabit a single tree. There, they remain for the entirety of winter until their compasses flip direction once again.

But just how do these monarchs find their way to a place they've never been? Their magic is actually not entirely understood; somehow, they utilize an internal map passed down from their great-great-grandparents. Monarchs also follow the light of the sun and rely on an inner magnetic compass on cloudy days. They even catch rides on air currents, sometimes flying a mile high in the sky. This Super Generation's journey is quite a fascinating sight to see. Witnessing their flight has been compared to rivers in the sky or sometimes even described as storm clouds.

Spiritual Symbolism

Why am I sharing all of this with you? Well, the incredible and unique journey of the monarchs, which spans multiple generations, carries a lot of spiritual significance. You could even say that the journey of the monarch butterfly mirrors our own spiritual evolution. This may be why I have always been fascinated by them, or perhaps the reason they have consistently appeared to me and are making their presence known once again!

Much like humans, monarch butterflies embark on a journey that takes them into the unknown. They fly forward, not knowing where they are going but fully trusting that when their journey ends, the next generation will pick up where they left off. This is an enormously powerful concept. Not only that, but remember each butterfly must always begin as a caterpillar. Each and every one must break down and shed what is no longer needed in order to reach their ultimate potential and destination. There is no shortcut to their growth! And although unrecognizable as their former caterpillar selves, the most essential parts remain within the butterfly.

Instinctually and perhaps without even consciously knowing, with every migration period, each generation moves the entire species forward, leading to a *Super Generation* that will eventually complete the process. It's the selfless act of the generations before the *Super Generation* that blindly takes action.

They don't know where the journey will lead them, but they have faith that the process will benefit the grandbaby butterflies they will never even have the chance to meet.

Our own spiritual journey is a lot like this migration. This pattern can be seen in our one lifetime, our many lifetimes (if you believe that), and the lifetimes of our ancestors as well as our descendants.

In some ways, we are all like monarch butterflies. Each of us is on our own unique journey, having to rely on blind faith and trust (at many times in our lives) that we are moving in the right direction, not only for ourselves in the present, but also for future generations. Similarly, we too will break down and go through not one, but sometimes several metamorphoses in a single lifetime! And the key to our transformation is within the parts we are leaving behind. We can't always see the bigger picture, and we don't get to know what the final outcome will be, but we have to trust that it is all for a larger purpose, one that extends far beyond our individual lives.

And just as the monarch butterfly follows the light of the sun, we too are guided by a light, the light that connects us to something far greater. We each have a deep knowing and a voice that guides us, whether we realize it or not. Intuitively, when we are on the right path, we can feel it. We are living in alignment. Life is more joyful and intentional. On the other hand, when we veer off course, we feel depressed, lost, and disconnected from ourselves. We are devoid of joy, and life feels like it is happening to us with little to no control over it. I think we can learn to see this detour as a gift too. And if we are brave enough to listen to that inner voice and trust the pull of our own butterfly compasses, we can always get on the right path again.

And as you keep moving forward, trusting yourself, you too will eventually make it to the *Super Generation* stage. There you will feel connected to your highest spiritual truth and calling, feeling confident to raise the little ones that will or have already come through you (if you choose), knowing that they will fly faster and farther than you ever have! And in living from this place of alignment, you too will take flight to newly discovered places and experiences, beyond your wildest imagination! Not only for the benefit of your singular life but also for your children, grandchildren, great-grandchildren, and great-great-grandchildren!

Monarchs in History

Not surprisingly, the beauty and magic of monarch butterflies has been recognized all throughout history. Their significance is interwoven within different cultures and religions all around the world. Scientists have proven that these magical winged creatures have been in existence for up to 200 million years, so it's no surprise that there would be a myriad of stories told about them.

For example, in Native American culture, monarch butterflies represent hope in the future as well as abundance and health. In general Christianity, monarch butterflies are seen as a symbol of foretelling and spiritual transformation. Within Catholicism in particular, monarchs are seen as a symbol of rebirth. Some people even believe that a monarch butterfly sighting is a sign that you are on the right path to achieve your goals.

As you can imagine, Mexico specifically has a very special relationship with monarch butterflies since the land is part of their yearly migration. Each year, the monarchs make their arrival around Día de los Muertos, the Day of the Dead—a very well-known Mexican celebration in which the souls of deceased relatives are welcomed back on Earth. Legend says that these butterflies are actually the physical representation of the departed visiting during these holy days to provide comfort to those loved ones left behind.

So not only is the monarch butterfly a symbol of wonderment and inspiration in present times, but it is also an ancient creature that has been revered by cultures across history.

Butterfly Sightings

In the case of my own life, there have been many prominent times where monarch butterflies have appeared to me. When they have a message or want to make their presence known, I will see them everywhere. It is happening again now. It feels like the butterflies are calling to me to tell you *their* story. To share their magic in a way that also supports the freeing process of telling you my own story, which I hope will in turn inspire you to share yours and find a newfound freedom of your very own.

Have you ever noticed signs during big phases in your life? I can relate to almost all of these cultural and spiritual meanings of butterflies.

I have had monarch butterflies seemingly follow me across states in my travels. They will appear to me during the hardest as well as the happiest times. When I see them now, they absolutely give me a sense of feeling supported and a nudge that I am on the right path. It's such a great reminder to me that life truly is always guiding you—you just have to pay attention!

I have been through several major transformational periods throughout my life, and if you have been called to read this book —I am sure you have too. And when you think about it, that's what life is meant to be. A series of cycles leading to a great "unbecoming," as I like to call it. Between birth and death we pick up a lot that we don't need along the way that we must learn to shed in order to remain connected to the core of who we are and to maintain the clarity to stay on the path to where we are going.

Butterflies do not just exist; they are created quite literally by breaking down to almost nothing and emerging into unbelievably new, never-before-seen, indescribable beauty—just like you and me. I am so grateful for butterflies that remind us that out of the darkest of places, the most radiant beauty emerges. In fact, have you ever realized that *all* magic gets created in the dark? Flowers begin as seeds buried in the dirt, away from the bright sun. In fact, one of my favorite flowers, the lotus, emerges from murky mud pristine and pure. Butterflies we know are born from the dark chrysalis. Stars emerge from a cold, dark cloud of dust and gas. And, of course, there is also you and I, born from the dark womb. The big question is, will you dare trust yourself to remain connected to your light? To the spark of the divine, that radiance that has always been there since the moment life began for you and even before that?

Embrace Your Transformation

Butterflies are the epitome of change. They remind us that total transformation is not only possible but necessary to reach our destination and that the beautiful parts of who we are remain within. Their appearance also represents the change of the seasons in more ways than one, and I invite you to welcome them into this season of your life. Monarchs travel in groups which are magically referred to as a kaleidoscope, and they know that their individual journeys are an integral part of the fabric of the whole. We are not meant to go at it alone, we *need* each other. This is important because we can see how breakdowns occur when this is not the case in our own lives. For those of us who have not experienced the feeling of safety that allows us to soar within our own birth families, you may notice that it leads us to become hyper-independent or codependent, both which are unhealthy.

These traits can show up as appearing fiercely independent on the outside, yet more often than not feeling helpless and defeated on the inside. You're self-sufficient, not of your own choosing, and you crave having the stability of someone to depend on. You love real, authentic people. Your life was one of lies, secrets, and confusion, that the truth feels like waves washing over you, revealing indescribable clarity and leaving behind a sense of peace and security. Although it appears that you are a "what you see is what you get" type of person, at the same time, you have all these beautiful layers that you keep hidden, hoping others can see and acknowledge them so that you no longer feel misunderstood or feeling like you do have to hide. You have a big heart, but you are afraid to get *too attached*. You test others' love for you, but it does not come from a place of manipulation. Rather, it is an instinct of trying to protect yourself from the pain of losing it.

If you find yourself with the highest honor of now being, becoming, or thinking of becoming a mother yourself and you feel fiercely adamant about not re-creating the toxic patterns you grew up with for your children, I invite you to find yourself in the pages of this book. If you are a woman who wants to heal or is scared to have children for this very reason, my purpose is to be an avenue of support for you. If you are someone still dealing with the ramifications, consequences, effects, impact, and so on of your trauma, I get it. And I share my story for *you*.

I want you to know that I can relate to many of the challenges you're going through. If you feel disconnected from yourself and from others, know that it won't be forever. If the idea of being related to your birth family makes you feel like a fish out of water or even makes your skin crawl—I completely get it. If you know that you are not showing up in your life the way you want to for yourself, your kids, your partner, or anyone else who is important to you, I see you. I acknowledge you. If you know that there is a life so much bigger just waiting around the corner, you are not alone and you are not wrong—there is!

If you have that gnawing feeling that something needs to change (maybe you're aware of your trauma and can see it showing up in your relationships or interactions and want to put an end to it, but you can't exactly see the solution just yet), I validate you. You are not crazy. You have every right to feel the way you do! If you have a deep fear that you cannot remember who you were before the trauma, I am holding space for you—you absolutely can and you will. If you feel like you can't connect back to the core of who you are, I promise you that is not true. If your identity is encapsulated and feels permanently defined by your trauma and you feel like you no longer know who you are without it, I guarantee that you are not doomed to be tied to it forever. Know that you can never be truly lost nor can you ever be irreparably broken. It is okay to set down that pain once and for all, and let it go!

It doesn't matter what stage you are at in your life or where you are on your journey, if it feels like there is a problem, there is also a solution. I know that from my own experience. In fact, if a problem exists, so does the answer—it is just the truth of the life we were born into—even if it feels impossible right now. Finding your way back to the light, *your* light, and knowing there's no way to truly be disconnected from it, is essential. Understand that what you need to shed or set down or release or remove is the perception of your own darkness. Your judgment of it. Darkness is not bad; it's quite powerful, as you are already learning. And not being afraid to look at it? Well, that is where the magic happens! What do you need to rediscover? What do you need to completely remove or perhaps merely consider, acknowledge, and reframe? What if there is no part of yourself or your story that you cannot pour love into or be afraid of anymore? Who would you be then?

You are on your own butterfly journey, and it will be unique to you. Every butterfly's transformation is her own and I'm not going to tell you that it is going to be easy or perfect, but I do promise that there is a light at the end of that seemingly endless, dark tunnel—and if I can do it, so can you!

Birth, death, re-creation—it's the cycle of life and it really is something to be celebrated. Yes, death can be looked at as darkness. While we hate to look at it and love to fear it, can you find the beauty in death as well? Death is essential for new life. We live in a dualistic world, a place where you cannot have the light without the dark. The more you push away the fear, the more you're actually amplifying it while simultaneously shutting out the joy. I am here to teach you how to integrate the two and feel whole again (because you already are), and I couldn't be more honored to share my journey with you. Take what resonates in the pages to come and leave the rest, because learning to trust yourself again will be of the highest priority.

Turn Your Journey into Your Purpose

The journey of the monarch butterfly speaks to the core of what I do in *all* of my work. The entirety of my life has felt like a healing journey (maybe you feel that way too), even though I haven't always been aware of it, I have always been drawn to share that healing with others. Anything I learned, I wanted others to know it too. If it helped me, I would want to help you. I'd want to scream it from the rooftops to anyone who would listen!

There was a phase in my healing journey where I was all about positive thinking. I thought I could happy-think my way into anything. But now I know that you simply cannot bypass the shadow work—the things we are afraid to look at. It is just as or even more important. I believe that is the key to healing. In fact, contrary to what I once thought, to be happy all the time is not the goal, but to be at peace is. To find peace amongst any chaos life has thrown or is throwing at you. To be the thermostat and not the thermometer.

I also realized that when people are not ready to face their own transformation, they will hate the thing that reminds them of the work they are refusing to do. People will always find their way in their own time, even if that means never finding it. It is not our job, nor can we do the work for others. Some people will never have the strength to look at that pain and that's okay. We have to accept it because that is out of our control. To be honest, looking within, facing yourself—while it holds all the power—is downright scary! It is the hardest, most rewarding work you will ever be called to do, and if you have that calling, trust me, you are capable.

I also learned as I got older, and a little wiser, that the best way to lead others is to do so by example. In fact, the more I embodied the transformations happening inside me, the more people gravitated toward me. The more they wanted to know just what I was doing. Being in my energy made them feel better, which would surprise me at times until I was ready to own that I had changed.

I began creating. I started sharing. To empower others to use their voice, I had to be willing to use my own, with purpose, and that is exactly what I slowly began to do. Life has a funny way of always falling into place. Everything is always in alignment, even during the times life feels like a mess, and I still have to remind myself of this. It's paradoxical, I know, but this too is a universal truth. When you veer off course, there's an internal global positioning system, a.k.a. GPS, that always reroutes you, and the detour ends up being such an essential part of the voyage. Other times, like a butterfly, total deconstruction is necessary and the *only* way to arrive at the next stage.

As I expanded as a person, so did my calling. And my work was not only healing to others, but it was also part of my own healing journey. We teach what we are called to master. I worked with girls because for many years I was healing that inner little girl through my work with them. As I integrated and felt more whole and confident, more and more women were drawn to the courses I was teaching. It took me almost three years to write this book. I left it and came back to it many times in its own birthing process. And while I wrote this book before I created my newest program for women, as I came back to edit it and the program was being brought to life, I realized that there were so many similar themes running through both! Life is amazing when you really look at it. And that's the trouble with it when you're really in the thick of things—it really is so difficult to see the forest from the trees. But as you stop to take a step back and look at where you've been, where you're going becomes clearer, and you can really appreciate how far you've come too. Trust it!

This book is the story of my own butterfly journey. Its purpose is to guide you to your personal power. It's true what they say, the best teachers don't give you the answers, they only show you where to look. And so, in sharing my own story, I'm not telling you "this is how you do it," but rather sending you the clear message that you can trust yourself and you are more powerful than you give yourself credit for. All the answers can be found inside of yourself, but we do need others to help us see the things we can't or have simply forgotten from time to time.

After one of the darkest nights of my life, I woke up realizing that all the decisions I had made up to that point were through the lens of my trauma (and let me tell you that was a scary realization); however, it also allowed me to acknowledge that all of my prior experiences had brought me to that very crucial and pivotal moment. Healing will happen when it's meant to. You can trust that the next step will always reveal itself to you when you're ready and not a moment sooner.

I have been helping others find their voice amidst the darkness and connect back to themselves before I was even conscious of what I was doing. It is now the clear purpose and intention of my life. And with that, I'd like to welcome you to your next step!

Approaching Metamorphosis

I am a first generation American, trauma survivor, mother, educator, healer, and magic maker, but none of those labels mean anything, because at the end of the day I see myself as a channel. A vehicle to take my experiences and transmute them into tools to help others.

I see the work I do is as transformational to women and girls as metamorphosis is to monarch butterflies, but I've never shared the story of my own evolution so openly and so detailed until now. In the chapters to come, you will learn my personal story of transformation and growth. But more importantly, you will discover a way to connect back to your own inner strength. Look at this book as an initiation into your own unbecoming and as a reminder that you are the source of your own power, even if it has felt grossly overshadowed at times—even if it feels that way now! I share with you my own journey in the hopes that you will be inspired by it.

As I got older, one of the many ways in which I tried to make sense of my life and understand the impact of my pain was through reading books. There were times in my life that I practically lived at the library. Whenever a new brick wall showed up (and trust me, at times they seemed never-ending), I would find a book that I thought could help. I knew that if I read about someone overcoming the same problem I was facing or worse, then there was hope that I could do it too. I found myself in the stories of others. So, my prayer, my intention, is that I can be that for you as well.

I'm also going to share with you how I had to quite literally break down to goo (mentally, emotionally, and physically) and rebuild myself. I had to learn to trust myself again and again by connecting back to the source of my power, and transforming into the beautiful butterfly I have always meant to be. I had to come to the realization that every setback, obstacle, and pain point was pushing me into the next stage of my evolution. In fact, those were the biggest clues! So, whether you're at the egg, larva, pupa, emerging butterfly, or adult stage, there's always a reason to keep going. When you feel crushed, it's easy to feel worthless, but this is a reminder that you matter. Don't give up. Life demands this of you. So much more is waiting for you on the other side—I know you can feel it . . . trust that!

Egg

Life before Life

We are more than just who we are. We are a product of all those that came before us and all of their experiences too. My parents were Italian immigrants. My mother was born in Alcamo, Sicily, in 1943. She is the middle child of five although two sisters who came before her passed away very, very young. Her family was poor and, until this day at the age of seventy-seven, she will cry if she tells the story of how she didn't even have shoes to wear on her feet as a child. If and when my mom opens up, which is rare, there is a very sad little girl inside, one who also believes her life was arduous.

My father was born in Siracusa, Sicily, in 1941. On the other side of the island. A lot of his life is unclear to me. The one thing that was evident was that one by one each of his parents' seven children found ways to leave the nest as early as possible. Some through marriage. Some through a life of crime. My father, the baby, left by joining the military—the Italian Navy.

The pair both made their way to New York City. Their paths inevitably crossed in 1968 when my mother was working in a sweat factory in Manhattan, making men's suits with my father's older brother. My mother was friends with my future uncle's oldest daughter (my father's niece), and she introduced the two.

After a brief three-month courtship, they became engaged and by early the following year they were married. I have tried to go down memory lane with my mother, curious as to what she saw in a man like my father and if there were any signs of the type of man he would later become. But the very little of what she told me has painted a different picture than the harmful father I would come to know.

My mother, a woman of little words and much less open heartedness, explained that it was a whirlwind romance and that she was head over heels in love. She said that he showered her with lots of affection and gifts, which clearly had her sold on his goodness. On the outside, they were an incredibly stunning couple. I mean, they were gorgeous, model material—both of them. But their insides would reveal quite the opposite.

I never did get my father's side of the story pertaining to their "romance." He lavished on her with amorous gestures when I was much younger. In fact, that still makes up some of the very few happy memories I had with him. He would take me shopping to buy her the biggest box of chocolate he could find or one of those humongous, oversized greeting cards. I still have the green Duncan yo-yo he bought me on one of our outings (one of the very few gifts I ever remember him giving me). But people who knew my dad and my mom at the time shared that his only reason for getting married was to remain in the United States. (I guess add this to the list of things I will never really know.) I have heard that he had someone he loved dearly in Sicily, but for reasons unknown the marriage wasn't meant to be. There were stories that my mother had a similar connection back in her hometown, but as fate would have it, these two ended up together.

My parents went on to bear a son, my older brother and only sibling. It was traditional in Italian families to name the firstborn son after the paternal grandfather, and the firstborn daughter after the paternal grandmother. My older brother was truly the apple of both their eyes. If anyone got the good parts of this union, it was him (or so I thought). The perfect son, the golden child—there was nothing he could do wrong. He got the love; he got the praise. He even got the bigger allowance. He got the recognition, the support, and the illusion of being seen. He received the accolades. And if he tried something they approved of (like that one season he played soccer), he got the cheering on the sidelines too. My brother grew up to become their counsel on all things famiglia.[1] He came out with a different view of my parents than I did and a different type of trauma, yet trauma nonetheless—I always find it fascinating how that happens. How two people living in seemingly identical environments can have two drastically different experiences.

Birthed into Survival Mode

Then I came, four and a half years later. According to tradition I should have been named after my paternal grandmother, Carmela; however, my father being the youngest of

---

1. *Famiglia* is the Sicilian word for "family"

seven children, you can just imagine how many Carmelas were already in existence by the time I came along. So, after some disagreeing, my parents settled on naming me Carmine after a prominent saint in my father's town—La Madonna del Carmine or Our Lady of Mount Carmel—which took on much greater meaning later on in my life. Being that in the United States Carmine was a name reserved for boys, I did endure some teasing and over time dropped the "e" at the end—hence the unique spelling of my first name.

My brother and I were born to two completely different parents (which is a common occurrence). Actually, they say you can never be the same parent twice. With each child that is born, you yourself are different—you're older, you're wiser, and maybe you're not as worrisome. In my case, it felt like they were even more dysfunctional. It would be expected that my parents were dissimilar parents to me than they were to my brother, but these parenting differences could cut walls. They were so starkly contrasting that it was painful to watch and experience by both of us, although I always felt I got the shorter end of the stick.

My life was a struggle from the start. I was slammed right into survival mode from the moment of conception, it seems. My mother has mentioned that she bled throughout her entire pregnancy with me. That she feared for my life early on. I am not sure how well she was being treated by my father at the time, but it was clear life was challenging for both of us.

Also came the fact that I was a girl. I was the youngest child, the youngest and *only* girl, in an Italian family. If what the mafia movies depict is the truth, I would have been adored, and spoiled—the quintessential princess. Ahhhh, but nothing could have been further from the truth. In fact, what I became and what I felt like was a tool for my father's pleasure. A possession. A plaything. A target of physical/mental/emotional abuse from the time I was born. Daddy's little girl never took on a more sick and twisted meaning than it did for me. I still cringe at the signature line in all his greeting cards to me. He always signed them, "Love, Daddy hugs and kisses, xoxo."

But I was just a child. Prepubescent. I had no idea what type of family I was born into. I had no idea the things that were happening to me were wrong. All I knew was that I didn't like it. Not only did I not like it, it repulsed me. As I got old enough, the only driving force in my life was to avoid it—my father—at all costs.

I did try later on to receive the love, the recognition, the accolades reserved for my brother. In fact, I would have loved any kind of attention. I played softball and volleyball. I was met with, "Girls don't play sports!" Believe it or not, not one of my family members came to a single game. I tried stealing from my father. Surely taking his money would get some attention. I tried breaking my necessities, things like my glasses. I began hurting myself. I tried slamming my arm in the sliding closet doors at my nonna's house, once hoping to break it and maybe get a little attention. I got beat up by my first boyfriend (that one was not on purpose). I was the first to graduate college. But good or bad, what I did didn't seem to matter. I even got diagnosed with early stages of cervical cancer as a young adult, but still none of my family was anywhere to be found. No matter what the circumstance was, I did not seem worthy of their attention, support, or least of all protection.

Again, it's hard getting anything out of anyone in my family. It's like the knowledge, memories, and wall of secrets were ironclad, which is interesting considering the way my brother and I turned out. I, the truth teller, and he, a heart-on-his-sleeve kind of person. He will talk and talk to no end. God bless him.

As a family, we never spoke of anything of importance. It was like you had to go at life's problems on your own even if those problems were created at home in the first place. My mother and I never had very clear communication between us. Maybe it was the barrier of language? But Sicilian was the only language I knew as a young child. In fact, I would not master English until I started school and, even then, my early classes were bilingual (English/Italian). Could it be because she didn't have much of an education and remained for the most part illiterate? Or maybe it was just because she was so shut down and disconnected emotionally that I never felt that she could relate to me in any real way.

I felt invisible. That was the essential belief I took on about myself: I was an invisible, worthless piece of shit. Now I like to fantasize that this was not my parents' intention. I would like to think that they didn't go into parenthood hoping to traumatize their one and only daughter—their baby. I know that I, personally, had the best of intentions going into motherhood—and I know that I made mistakes anyway. But needless to say, it has been a *very difficult* journey being born into a family with whom I had little to no comprehension and still do not.

I grew up feeling like my mother genuinely didn't like me. And in retrospect I can honestly say that I believe she didn't like the attention my father gave me because she communicated that (in her roundabout or not-so-roundabout ways). I remember in one of our very few conversations her saying: "When he was interested in you, he wasn't interested in me."

I am sure she would deny this statement today but, because my mother was a woman of few words, the minimal things she did say stuck with me. In fact, they are burned and etched in my mind, unable to be erased.

I remember as a little girl sitting on our velvety orange couch covered in plastic, the living room dimly lit, begging her to leave my father. She clearly and calmly stated that she was married in front of God and she took her vows seriously and she could not leave him. But she never seemed appalled at the notion. She never said: "Where in heaven did you get such a suggestion?" She never asked why I would need her to leave him. Because she knew. If there is one thing I know for sure, it's that she knew who my father really was and how he violated me.

Ironically, my mother did not seem to stay in the marriage because of some sort of obligation or promise as she implied. In fact, now that it has been years since my brother and I have moved out, with families of our own, she remains married and loyal. She loves and serves him until this very day, continually putting aside everyone's needs, including her own, to make sure that his are met daily and without fail.

And people have justified this behavior to me over the years. It's just what women did—they stayed. It was their culture, their this, their blah, blah, blah—but guess what? I don't give a fuck. Clearly something in my mother is also broken to have allowed this to happen, but even that awareness does not help me to comprehend how she could permit such abhorrent behavior to take place. I would never allow my child or children to be hurt and mistreated in the most profane way—not ever.

And my mother did not just remain married to this man. My mother loved him (at least that's what she called it), obeyed him, and allowed him to talk down to her and steal any hope for goodness in ALL of our lives. On some days when I have compassion for her (I still work on this), I wonder if maybe she's just a victim too. And in many ways, I am sure she is and if we dug deep enough, we might find my father was some victim of trauma as well. As children I am sure they both were because ugliness doesn't come out of nowhere—not usually. Most trauma gets passed down from generation to generation. What my parents displayed for my brother and I was not a pure love, not in my opinion, and the relationship they had with one another was a codependent one, the same kind I would, unfortunately, be doomed to repeat.

I never thought my dad was one of those typical abusers like I saw on television. He never told me to lie. Or did he? I don't remember him saying things to me like you saw in those after-school specials: "This is our little secret" or anything like that. Later on, I would be told he was "sick"—so I believed it. He didn't know what he was doing, right? This was the explanation I was given. There were actually two theories floating around. One was about an ear surgery my father underwent to address what was described to sound like a swimmer's ear. Apparently, the surgery affected part of his brain and turned him into a sex-crazed maniac, which consequently made him aroused by children. The second was around a trip he took to Italy with my mother. Allegedly the turbulence was so bad on the flight that he feared for his life, and he was never the same after that. Somehow turning to pedophilia seemed a logical consequence.

While I have no doubt both experiences could have changed him in a profound and lasting way, for so many reasons I am sure you will piece together on your own, neither of these events is the reason my father sexually abused me or the reason my mother allowed it to repeatedly take place.

My father ran the household finances so meticulously, down to the very last penny. If you took a dollar from his stash, he knew. In the dynamics between him and my mother, it was evident—he was head of household. Dad was the boss. He kept up with the world at large: politics, the weather, sports, and the latest Ms. America Pageant. And my father was funny, like really funny—he was charismatic and charming and most people liked him. In many ways he appeared normal, which made it hard for me to buy into the theory that he was so "sick" that he could not control his sexual urges over a child.

The story felt so utterly incongruent. It also felt like an insult to my intelligence. And maybe that's why I just couldn't "get over it" like they asked me to repeatedly because it just didn't and doesn't make sense, but could it ever? As an adult I would learn my experiences were unfortunately not uncommon. Plenty of people in the world do bad things and fly completely under the radar. Despite this, it could never really make real sense to me because he was supposed to be my dad! It felt that way then, and it feels that way now.

I was also never validated and my experiences were never acknowledged. This is the main reason that I would lose faith and trust in myself and continuously stay in things that were so evidently unhealthy. But I also remember my father's words imprinted in my mind—and I do pray they remain burned in his forever along with the memory of what he took from me—because anytime I tried to speak up, anytime I tried to voice my truth, he told me that I would kill her. He told me I would kill my mother with these lies that I was "making up."

And you know what? There was a part of me that believed him. He put fear in my little heart with that statement. I didn't see it as manipulation then, but I do see it now. This was his way to make sure what he was doing to me *did* remain a secret, although it didn't work—and it didn't actually matter because they both knew, my mother and brother, and they believed his protection was more important than mine.

Inferno

The home that I lived in as a child was located in the Bushwick section of Brooklyn, New York. We lived on the second floor of a three-family tenement building my parents owned. My cousins lived next door. Although surrounded by so-called "family," I felt isolated and in a hell-like existence on the daily.

Each day, my one and only goal was survival. I know it seems dramatic but as a kid growing up in it, that's how it felt. It was downright scary and confusing. For me, my life simply became a mission of avoiding being alone with my father at all costs, and that was a lot of stress for a little girl especially when the man was always home! He had stopped working and was on full disability due to his mental illness and/or unresolved trauma right around the time I was born. I would also internalize this timeline to mean something about my birth was what made him sick or triggered his trauma. This had to be my fault.

Young girls should be worried about—nothing really. They should be frolicking free with pigtails flopping in the air, just learning and being curious about life. But this was so far from reality for me (despite having pigtails at times).

I was indeed learning every day, learning lessons no little girl should ever know. I was learning that I was unsafe in an unsafe world. In fact, I was not even safe in my own body, a space that I would separate myself from for years to come, not realizing just how difficult it would be to later come home to. By the same token, however, this is precisely what allowed me to survive the experience and the trauma of being sexually abused and assaulted over and over again.

I have no recollection of when it began nor can I give you a concrete time of when it ended. All I can say is that over the span of what felt like at least fourteen years, my father was my abuser. I would also come to understand that my mother was in many ways perhaps worse than he was (if you can believe that). My brother, unintentionally and unconsciously always teetering on what side to be loyal to, eventually chose them too, which crushed my little girl heart and would for a very, very long time.

You abide by the family code. This was just known. Every family has its own set of unspoken rules; some are just more sinister than others. Ours was an unspoken vow of silence that covered up a shame that we were all experiencing in one way or another, including my father.

Every day was a mission to get home without waking up the man who was equally responsible for giving me life and destroying it. He slept a lot those days. He slept and seemed to wake up only to terrorize me. There was nothing in my life I could depend on with certainty except for uncertainty. Every day when I came home from school, I didn't know what I would be walking into. Would my dad be completely naked and aroused just waiting for me? Or would my brother be home by some miracle and keep him from "bothering" me—because for someone who was so "sick" he was well enough and in his right mind enough to only abuse me when no one else was around.

My father was a very ill man indeed, although to me he was just *my dad*, and while I knew his actions made me feel very icky and uncomfortable inside, I truly had no way of knowing how abhorrent this behavior was because this was just *my life*.

I spent what felt like all of my days trying to make sense of this crime and tragedy. The violent removal of my innocence, and the wondering why so many people have lived through many of the same things I did, including many of my own family members. How do these abusers get away with it? I wondered, back then, who knew in my extended family and said nothing—too many, I would later find out. I wondered why the man not only responsible for my life but also entrusted with the honor of guiding it, single handedly shattered it.

What would make the man given the privilege of protecting me hurt me in such a profoundly violating way? What could have happened in his own life to view me as nothing more than a source of his perverted pleasure? What gene was he lacking that overrides a man's true nature of wanting to protect the women and children in his life?

The truth is, I will never know. I have come to terms with the reality that there are some facts of our lives, life in general, that are truly incomprehensible. Why do bad things happen to good people? Honestly, I think there are some things we are not meant to know and just have to trust that nothing really goes unpunished. And while I will die with these questions unanswered and although so much healing has been done, I don't think anyone ever ceases to grieve such a profound loss, and that's okay too. That's just what it is—a loss. The loss of never having a father, the loss of innocence, the loss of feeling safe or any semblance of security. It was the loss of a mother too, of a cohesive family unit. The loss of feeling valued or worthy of protection. The loss of the protective big brother. The loss of me trusting myself, trusting my experiences, and feeling like I could be heard, believed, and eventually saved.

That salvation never came. No one came to rescue me. I was left to deal with such grotesque matters all alone until I was old enough to somewhat face the reality of my life. But I would live in denial and dissociation for a very, very long time. Wanting so desperately to have a normal family, I did what my mother unknowingly modeled for me in her silence; I went along with the dysfunction for a long time. Too long. I thought I could fix what was so irreversibly broken, but there are some things not meant to be, nor are they worthy of being repaired.

My early home life, my experiences with my father, spilled out onto every other area of my life outside of that. It was inevitable. How could it not? You don't live through something like that and come out unscathed. You become very, very broken on the inside (at least it feels that way). But that's one thing that I have learned: You are never irreparably broken—the human spirit, your resiliency, has capabilities beyond your wildest imagination. I am proof of that. If you're here reading these words, so are you!

Silence as the Real Sin

I am not sure if it was the mere fact that I was biologically a girl, but that simple truth seemed to get me a lot of different treatment than the boys in my family—at least that was the reason I told myself and a belief I internalized. Within my immediate family, my brother was king. I, on the other hand, was invisible. Among my extended family (we spent the most time with my mother's younger brother's family), I was the only girl cousin of the bunch, so I always felt left out. My nonna—my mother's mother—was the only person who made me feel like a star simply for being myself.

I remember sitting on my front stoop one evening with my brother and his best friend. They had to be about seventeen or eighteen at the time. My brother said to me, "You know you can't say anything about Dad or he would get into a lot of trouble." His friend did not say a word and he was someone I really respected and looked up to. I even had a crush on him at one time. Surely, he knew what the right thing to do was. I know my brother crucified himself for those words for a long time afterward—maybe he still does. They gutted me too.

I didn't understand how fucked up it really was then, in the moment, because of the code of silence—it's just what you did. You covered up in order to keep from bringing the family embarrassment or shame—*vergogna* is what it was called in Sicilian. It was worse than any childhood sex crime apparently. I didn't realize how I was always being silenced in subtle but profound and long-lasting ways. My dad told me my silence would save my mother, my brother said my silence would save my father, but who would save me? What was my silence doing to me?

The crazy thing is, I bought into it too. I kept the secret. None of my friends knew except for my bestest, closest friend. And even so—this is how you know the instinct to cover up trauma runs deep—she never said, "You should tell someone!" And so, I too would cover up the family shame. I would protect their images, their reputation, and I guess mine too. How embarrassing, humiliating, and violating. When I told friends years later, they recalled me constantly being on high alert. They didn't understand why we made a beeline from my front door straight to my room and then locked the door behind us. They had no idea why I was always yelling at my dad. When my friend came and visited me after having my first daughter, she didn't know why my father was not allowed to see my baby. Whenever I was around them (my birth family)—I was not safe. I had to protect myself and protect those I loved. What an utterly exhausting way to live.

This was an unspoken lesson. I was taught that my experiences did not matter. It was easier to sweep it under the rug than to deal with it. If I would just shut up, it would all just go away. Ironically, as a young child, I actually didn't have the words to share what was happening. I tried but the words were more like just cries and screams. My mother was aware of my father's character because this was not new behavior for him. In fact, years later I would discover that my father made sexual advances toward not one but many of his brother's daughters (his nieces), one who was a good friend of my mom's (the one who was responsible for introducing them)! Although she was a niece, she was contemporary in terms of their ages, but this advance he made towards her was when my mother was still in the honeymoon/engagement phase with my father! In fact, my father made a name for himself among his family. Aunts on his side of the family told their daughters not to be alone with him. I can't imagine how many other women and children my father would go on to be sexually inappropriate with. I was born almost ten years after their engagement. It's wild for me to think that maybe if someone said something to my mother, she would have ended the courtship and I would not be here today. But I have a strange feeling she solidified the relationship even while having that information or at least an inkling of it.

As a kid, I would yell and scream at my mom to leave my dad. Although I did not refer to him as my father. I would tell her her husband was crazy. She'd then yell at him for a few minutes and then all would be forgotten, and eventually we would cycle back into it again. In the quest to really understand how my experiences shaped me, I learned that I actually could not speak up. First, I had no frame of reference to describe what was happening—who could understand such sexual matters at that young age? Second, I didn't actually have the words to express it.

As a trained speech language pathologist I would later learn that there are two areas in the brain associated with speech and language. When I took a continuing education class on expressive therapy subtitled "Healing Trauma through Play, Art, Movement, and Storytelling," I was astonished when the course facilitator shared that trauma is stored in a part of the brain separate from the areas responsible for language. While this was surprising, it was also a huge light bulb moment for me and explained so much. She talked at length how trauma is stored in the same area where our emotions are stored and our creativity lies, which is why art, movement, and storytelling were so beneficial in releasing trauma and relearning new patterns. There were simply no words for me to access what I was experiencing in a literal way. So, when someone says they "have no words," believe them. This is why I fully stand by the fact that it is impossible to completely process trauma through talking alone. Talking is not enough.

Nonna's House

It's the darkest of nights that display the most radiant stars. In my world of darkness, Nonna absolutely represented the light.

Nonna's house was more familiar than home. It was just a three-minute walk from where I lived, but such a stark contrast to my regular life in every way. Although her home was just two blocks from mine, when I was stuck behind those closed doors, too young to leave on my own, we felt worlds apart. But even though Nonna and I did not live together, she was by far the most important and influential person in my little life. I can say without question that the time spent with her had the biggest, positive impact on me.

Nonna taught me the valuable lessons that affect so much of what I do today. Similar to what I learned at home, most of Nonna's lessons were also taught indirectly. As kids, we learn what is modeled for us, not so much what we are told to do. The actions of the adults in our lives make a far greater impact than their words, and, boy, was Nonna impactful. There was an enormous contrast between the two and Nonna's house energetically felt like a healthier place—a safe place. However, when you grow up in chaos, you are unfortunately taught to override the intuition that so naturally comes to you. Let this serve as a reminder that your inner wisdom has always been and will always be there. I felt it early on but I couldn't really explain it nor do anything about it. We know what *feels* best to us. Energy does not lie, and I truly believe positive is more powerful than negative, even though it does not feel that way when you are in it. So, although I spent more time with people who felt like they were destroying my spirit, Nonna's medicine overpowered the pain I was experiencing in many ways. I understand now that it was her demonstration of pure love that kept me from drowning in the dark abyss. I have only ever prayed and continue to pray that Nonna knows how much she single-handedly saved my life.

Nonna was technically an American citizen because she was born in New York City; however, her parents took her back to Sicily at the teeny tiny age of six months. When she returned to the United States decades later, she didn't speak a lick of English and had actually vowed never to learn, and she kept to that promise. In fact, when Nonna died, my willingness to speak her language slowly died too.

Nonna's name was Caterina—which is where I received my middle name from (middle names came from maternal grandparents). Unlike my family at home, she was always so happy to see me. I was anything but invisible to Nonna and her smile brightened up my whole world. The joy in her entire body when I came over was overflowing and constant. She was the definition of embodiment. Nonna was the one and only person I could depend on. She was my angel in every sense of the word. There was a sense of security in her home, in her presence, and in her arms.

Nonna lived in a three-story, six-family, brick apartment building. There were two apartments on each floor and hers was on the bottom right. As I got older I could freely visit on my own. Each time I arrived, it was the same routine. There were two doors to get through before the hallway that led to her apartment door. When I came over, I would ring the doorbell, and she would hold down the buzzer far too long every time, ensuring I had plenty of time to make it past each gateway. The second door had a big rectangular glass. When I got to it, I always saw Nonna, with her apartment door ajar, head peeking out, excited to see me. She was always there with the biggest smile on her face, and the first thing I always received was a big, long hug. "Carmelinaaaaa," she would say to me with such delight in her voice. As a kid, she was the only person that would ever call me that. (On the rare occasion someone calls me that today, I know it's Nonna still smiling at me.)

Nonna gave me her time—the most valuable commodity. She gave me the gift of her stories, which were like a window into her soul. She was always completely present and patient. I realize now that during all the times I spent with her, it was the way she loved and her powerful presence that kept me grounded in the truth of who I was and made me feel like I could finally rest. Her light and her ability to stand in it and share it with me kept me tethered to my own. Her ability to see mine and reflect it back was like a cloak of protection. Clearly Nonna knew pain and heartache, but she never placed any burdens on me. She seemed to find joy in what she had despite any hardships that came before. In this way Nonna modeled gratitude.

Nonna would tell stories of how difficult it was coming to America and not knowing the language. She would go to the store with empty milk cartons and broken eggshells to explain what she needed to buy. Although she was sixty-eight years my senior, she taught me the most about staying connected to the child within you. She shared how she was so poor growing up that she didn't have any toys and what she did have she was shown how to make with her own hands. She passed that on to me and taught me how to sew dolls from simple fabric. Nonna also had an almost life-sized doll that she gifted herself that sat on the center of her bed. She made dresses for that doll and brushed her hair every day. Looking back, it was almost like her way of giving love to the little girl inside of her as well as an opportunity to gift herself with something she never had as a child.

Funnily enough, it was Nonna who bought me my second and last Cabbage Patch Doll. It was a big deal to spend such a large amount of money on a toy. Remember the craze and how hard to find they were then? I still remember the picture of us and my new doll we took in front of the Rockefeller Center Christmas tree in New York City.

Nonna also shared her love through food. There was always an abundance of food at Nonna's house. God forbid you had eaten beforehand, there would be Nonna's disdain to deal with! One of the biggest insults to an Italian is to not eat their food. Each time she made me lunch or dinner, she would take out the same tablecloth. It was white with little blue flowers. She used this to cover up the fancy tablecloth underneath, even though it was already protected by plastic. I'm so grateful to say I still have and use that tablecloth today and utilize it often!

Nonna would engage in the same routine each and every time. She would take out the same plates and bowls. She made the same chicken cutlet and pasta, and although I didn't appreciate it then, she made the best meatballs around! The air would be filled with the scents of her culinary creations and they would linger on my clothes and hair hours later. I would come to understand that it was her consistency and routines that provided me with a sense of immense love and a feeling of safety in everything she did. Nonna was predictable and that felt so good to me.

Nonna's home was always so neat and tidy. She also ironed everything. Maybe it's because we didn't own dryers back then, and she certainly did not have one growing up, but she even ironed the bedsheets and underwear too! Nonna taught me how to hang clothes on the clothesline in size order (small items first). I still love the scent of clothes dried in the sunshine to this day!

Nonna also loved to crochet, and she was extremely talented. I remember Nonna sitting in a modest chair next to the window in her small dining room, sun piercing through, shining such a bright light on her as she worked to create magic with her hands. It was the perfect depiction of the angel she truly was to me. Nonna tried to teach me this skill, and I wish that I had had the attention span to learn or really believe that I could do it, but it seemed so complicated and intricate for my young, troubled mind. My home still remains adorned with so many of her creations.

Nonna poured into me. She told me my eyes were like two stars in the sky, and I believed her. I have no recollection of Nonna ever being detached or unable to connect. She was always in the moment. She is the definition of "you are love." Even in times of grief, for example, when Nonno passed away, Nonna shared her emotions so openly with me. The space was always clear. There were never any untruths or half-truths or any behavior that was misaligned with her words, and she is the reason that these things still make me feel secure in relationships today.

Nonna also taught me about magic and about life after death. She had been without her husband of over fifty years, and she often spoke of joining him. Nonna had zero fears or qualms about dying. She modeled that death was nothing to be afraid of, just a natural part of life. She also spoke about communicating with the other side in a way that made it also seem completely normal. Nonna told me she would be visited in the night often by figures who appeared at the foot of her bed. I'm not sure if they were ancestors, angels, or saints, but they told her that I wasn't okay and she couldn't leave me until I was okay. When she mentioned this to me, I didn't really respond. I didn't even know what to say or where to begin. I don't think she knew the extent of my pain or the nightmare I was living, and I never said anything.

Nonna also taught me about divinity, that we are a spark of the divine and connected to something bigger, outside of ourselves. Nonna did it through a Catholic framework, but it doesn't matter what you believe. It doesn't change what is irrefutably true—you are a part of something greater! She taught me to pray, which taught me about intention and having faith and the power of words and the energy behind them. Prayers are like wishes and in some ways manifestations. Nonna prayed the rosary every single day. She taught me the Our Father and the Hail Mary in Sicilian. She loved St. Joseph. I still hold dear to me an old Sicilian prayer she taught me to recite about St. Joseph. In fact, years later when I would have those "heart beating out my chest" panic attacks night after night after night, it was the Hail Mary and the Our Father that got me through, along with a simple phrase my former mother-in-law taught me: "This too shall pass."

Nonna also taught me about affirmations and words of protection—more magic. She loved the blessed Mother and every single time I left Nonna, she would repeat the following affirmation to me: "La madonna t'accumpagna." The literal translation of that is, "Mother Mary accompanies you." I didn't see it as an affirmation at the time, of course, just a sweet gesture or prayer of protection—but in hindsight, it was all three. These words would take on such greater meaning in my life. You see, Mary is representative of The Mother, the giver of life. She exists in all religious traditions, many that pre-date Christianity. My name is connected to her as well (if you recall). As I have grown as a person, my entire business and life have revolved around the magic and reverence of women, and more and more I see Our Lady guiding my way, reminding me that I have a purpose and that I am not alone. In fact, before the modern age, it has been said that the rosary, which is made up largely of the Hail Mary, was used to perform magic, pray for miracles, and a gateway to another world. It also reminds me of my favorite Beatles song where the lyrics speak to Mother Mary always being present even in times of despair not only to comfort but to share the insight to "Let It Be" and trust.

No matter what you believe or how alone you may have felt or feel, this is a reminder that you are not, have never been alone, and will never be. In fact, I am certain that the repetitive reminder that I was connected to a beautiful and powerful source far greater than me, was another reason I survived what I did.

And no matter how old Nonna was, she continued to do the things she loved. At the age of ninety-two she still walked to church every morning. This is the most beautiful symbolism I can think of when I think of Nonna. She lived a simple life, but she did so with such deliberate intention. She lived life in an orderly but beautiful and magical way. Her immense love still permeates to this day as she lives on through me, my children, and my work.

And the thing is, she didn't show up this way for everyone. I know she wasn't this person for her three children or her eight other grandchildren, but in some ways that was what made our relationship even more special. And when I think about it, maybe there was something about me that brought out healing for her, the best in her—imagine that! How beautiful to think I can be that for anyone when I spent most of my life believing it was I who brought out the worst in people—especially my father. Out of all of her grandchildren, we spent the most time together, and I am forever grateful that in someone's life I was number one. I'll never know if it was because she sensed I needed something or because she really loved me that much or both, but she gave this to me, and I would go on to spend so many years chasing that feeling again.

Family Patterns Emerging

As I got older and tried to pick up the pieces of my life and make sense of it, I realized there were some unhealthy patterns operating. Cycles that I kept falling into or were attracted to somehow, especially when it came to close relationships. One of them was something I later learned is referred to as triangulation. In triangulation, exclusion is used in order to achieve a desired outcome. The goal is to divide and conquer. Triangulation is a form of manipulation and involves the use of indirect communication, oftentimes behind someone's back.

This showed up in my family as the golden child/scapegoat dynamic. The golden child is idealized and can do no wrong. In my family this person was my brother. Although I don't think he realized this was manipulation on their part to get him to remain blindly loyal to them despite the heinous crimes being committed, it was and is a false sense of love and security. Don't rock the boat, and we will continue to support you. Don't call attention to the dysfunction occurring here, and we will still love you. The scapegoat (myself), on the other hand, was devalued and could only do wrong or just be altogether ignored. This led me to feel invisible and crazy, mainly when I tried to shed light on what was really going on.

This also revealed another toxic pattern: gaslighting. And while the term may be overused today, it truly is a form of psychological abuse. This happens when an individual's perception of reality is undermined by another person. The "that didn't happen" syndrome. When you repeatedly deny someone's reality you break down their sense of their own truth and their ability to trust in themselves. Even though you know what happened it makes you question yourself and your sanity and for me that seed was planted very early on.

The last two are enmeshment and disengagement. In enmeshment, the emotional bond between family members is intertwined without separation. There is no delineation between where one person ends and the other begins. It lays the groundwork for codependency. People who grow up in enmeshed families do not have a strong sense of self. They depend on others to feel validated and to feel self-worth. They don't function well alone and do not cultivate healthy levels of independence within relationships. This dynamic creates people that are unable to act and think separately from their family without the family making them feel as if they are betraying them. On the other hand—and at the opposite end of the spectrum—is disengagement: families that are completely emotionally separate from one another. In enmeshment it feels like blind loyalty, and in disengagement it's a lot more like isolation.

All of these patterns come as a result of insecurity. Insecure people are willing to manipulate others in harmful ways to get what they want, or feel a sense of control and security in a relationship. They create fake outward appearances to not let others know who they really are and what is actually going on. This is how I grew up and what was modeled for me and therefore would go on to recreate.

Larva

Ungrounded from the Start

Throughout my childhood, I felt unstable and constantly on shaky ground. It was not even feeling like the ground was ripped out from underneath me, but rather the feeling of it never existing in the first place and never knowing what was coming next—uncertainty. I felt fear. I had nightmares a lot as a child. It made sense that eventually the child within me who was silenced would come through me via nightmares once again.

As a kid, I dreamt of fires starting beneath the chairs in my family's dining room. These were recurring dreams. I often dreamt of my mother burning in what looked like some type of fireplace. I believe this revolved around my fear of losing her. I dreamt of burglaries and men violating me, which made sense as this was happening to me daily. Ironically, our house would later get robbed as well as get set on fire.

I felt anxious all the time, but I couldn't put a name to it then. Maybe because it was all just *normal.* I was always afraid of being alone, of getting lost, of losing my mother, or of her not returning someday. I remember hiding in those circular clothing racks when my mom would go shopping, and one day I couldn't find her when I got out and I vowed never to do it again. One day when I was walking home from school, I took a wrong turn somehow and felt so lost even though the school was still around the corner. Luckily a young boy helped me find my way. I would panic if it was past six o'clock on a week-day and my mother wasn't home from work. I'd go outside and see all the people walking around the corner getting off the train and hope to see her in the crowd. If she wasn't there, I'd wait until the next train came and the next group of people walking out until she finally got home.

Until this day, I still have dreams of getting lost when things are uncertain in my life or whenever I feel unsafe or in times of big change. In the dream, I'm in a place like a school or a party (the setting always changes). I'm trying to leave, but I never find my way out. When I was in the third grade, I got my own set of keys to the house. I was so worried about losing them that I would hold them in my hand all day in school. This is another clue that we're always getting messages.

As I got older and formed relationships outside my family, I was always trying to make sense of what true relating was. I doubted myself and I doubted the support of others. I was disconnected and detached and sometimes felt unable to really connect to anyone. I had a difficult time getting close to people. I was jealous and envious. I didn't believe anyone really liked or loved me for me, but at the same time had no idea who "me" was. I created triangulation amongst friends. I did things I am not proud of, like cause arguments within my friend groups so that I would be the chosen one. Because in my family I never felt chosen, I always longed to be.

For some reason, it was easier to be aware of this behavior with my friends and change (perhaps because the intimacy and true vulnerability isn't there—I'm not sure). By the time I was in high school, I had a beautiful core group of girlfriends, interestingly each and every one of them with their own trauma story. They became the family I consciously chose. I could relate to them and them me. I even had some amazing guy friends. They were respectful and honorable. Unfortunately, a core part of me believed I was not worthy of that, and those relationships always remained platonic even though some made declarations of wanting more. Later I would go on to attract other "friends" who created this type of dynamic, and I myself became the victim of this behavior, but when it came to friends it was so much easier to cut off and move on.

As I navigated the teen years, I felt shame, especially around my body. I was completely confused around all things sexual. How could things feel equally good and bad at the same time? I covered up my body because I learned that type of attention was dangerous. I hid my femininity. I always felt uncertain because there never seemed to be anything positive to depend on. If something good happened, I felt like it would not last.

I found it difficult to be present and in the moment, but at the same time, I could not think ahead. I felt frozen and not in my own body; dissociation was commonplace. As I got older, I would describe this feeling as a feeling of being buried alive. I lived in a state of constant stress inside, even though outwardly everything appeared to be . . . fine. And honestly, for the most part, I felt fine!

Although a lot of my life was spent disassociated, there's no real way I could have realized that then. Because so much of what I describe was, again, just my *normal*. I could not identify that nor put a label on it, but the incredible thing is that as you begin to heal, uncover, and unravel all that is not you, you come to the deepest parts of yourself and you really connect to the pain. For the first time ever, you will be able to tune in to that scared little girl and the feelings become so clear. The craziest thing is realizing that you have been operating from that very place all this time yet not have felt it! You cannot believe that you have been carrying this weight for so long that it really feels like a *part of you*.

Until I was a young adult and old enough to leave at will and move out, I felt completely and utterly alone and in a permanent state of confusion and in survival mode surrounding what was happening. There was no guidance, no help, no explanation, no nothing—nor would it ever come. At least not from the outside. It was from the inside that this illusion began to crumble many years later, and I am so absolutely grateful for that, although it was unbelievably terrifying at the time.

I'm not sure if I ever really saw my experiences and the people in my life for what and who they were, or if I was only seeing through the distorted lens of my worldview created by my dysfunctional childhood. I think it was and always has been a little bit of both and is the case for everyone. I think our experiences shape the way we see the world. But I also believe the purest parts of us are always there behind the clouded lens. It's our job to become aware of what is obstructing our view and slowly bring ourselves back to clarity.

I also believe we attract people who remind us of our light (the angels in our world), but we are also inevitably drawn to those people who feel familiar and trigger our pain. We end up re-enacting our childhood wounds with them with the hope of changing the story and getting the outcome we would have wanted. Especially in intimate relationships because it is in our most vulnerable state where our fears show up the loudest. Unfortunately, oftentimes, we end up creating more of the same trauma because subconsciously we are only trying to prove our own erroneous theories true. That certainly was the case for me. For example, because I felt inherently unworthy, I would subconsciously re-create this reality within my relationship. However when both people have the awareness of how their past is interrupting their present, these patterns can absolutely be shifted and healed within a healthy relationship dynamic. That is, if both partners are showing up and doing their own individual work. In my case, this would not come for a long time.

Looking back through new eyes, although I felt "fine" at the time, it was evident that I was literally seeping trauma through my pores. It was spilling out in every area of my life. How could it not? In every area of life, you have to relate to others, and people and situations bring up our stuff, so it was inevitable. Trauma gets stored in the body at the cellular level. Our body remembers everything even when the mind does not; therefore, those distressing experiences impact our actions and our relationships and reveal themselves there. If they remain unprocessed or stuck within us (which they especially do when abuse occurs while we are children because our brains are still forming), we repeat the cycle with others because these disturbing events create thought patterns and ways of relating, and they get imprinted within us.

There were plenty of consequences of my trauma, but when I think of the influence on my closest relationships, the following are some of the most powerful driving forces:

Number one: incongruence. Seeking love so desperately outside myself but with the belief that I was inherently unworthy of love. If that's not an uphill battle, I don't know what is. This led to a lot of people pleasing, going out of my way for others who would or could not reciprocate. Doing things for people who would never do the same for me. I struggled with that for years. That goes back to unworthiness and much, much difficulty with believing that I was deserving of receiving anything good. Because I felt undeserving, if something good happened, I would inevitably wait for the other shoe to drop.

Number two: having no boundaries. This was another major one. I had no idea what was a yes or a no for me. I knew the big no was obviously no unwanted sexual advances (in fact, this one became too rigid), but I knew nothing of what was a yes or no in other situations.

Number three: I lived in constant fear. I was in a hyper-aroused state most of the time without realizing it because again, this had become my norm. My nervous system was constantly in fight or flight or freeze/shutdown mode. It was hard for me to just relax and be, but I wasn't thinking about the next thing, which led me to not really think of the consequences of big decisions. I often made big life-altering decisions without thinking of any of the potential pitfalls.

Number four: I had no direction and no solid ground. I was like a chameleon and a leaf floating in the wind at the same time. I just became and did what people wanted me to be. My goals were based on what others thought I should be doing. I was so disconnected from myself. I had no idea who

I was or what my true desires were. I also was being pulled between my family's message—*find an Italian man, marry him and have babies*—and society's message—*go to college and start a career*—without ever stopping to ask myself what I really wanted. What a concept! I didn't know what I wanted in any aspect of my life so I pursued both of these avenues. I never really had dreams (except for being a backup dancer on *In Living Color* like JLo!) so things just felt like they were happening to me by default.

How did this all translate into the life I was creating? Well, the relationship we have with ourselves is one of the most important ones. Its role is so crucial, it's our foundation. It dictates all our many other relationships, which oftentimes becomes a mirror for us. What does that mean? It means the others we surround ourselves with are often a reflection of the way we really feel about ourselves inside. For example, if you find yourself not being loved or appreciated by those closest to you, ask yourself if you love and appreciate yourself. Are you being taken for granted? Then you might ask, where in your life have you taken yourself for granted? But the caveat is that not having good, solid, loving, and safe relationships with our caregivers distorts this reflection. This was my story. Because how can you have a good relationship with the self when those entrusted to your evolution squashed and stunted your growth? When those we love abandon us, we tend to abandon ourselves as well.

Whatever recurring theme you find in your external circumstance is usually a window into your internal landscape. In fact, it may not truly be happening in the way you think, but rather being deeply affected by your filter (the only setting you have), allowing no space to see it another way. It's like the quote by Anaïs Nin: "We don't see things as they are; we see things as we are."

Because my home was so devoid of love, safe touch, and safety in general, I would go on to hopelessly and desperately search for that in so many places and people outside of myself. However, you know how that story goes—the love we are looking for outside is really what we are wanting to feel inside. Consequently, I dated almost anyone (within reason) who gave me the time of day. I was looking for anyone to just be kind and love me. I had such low, low standards for myself. Ironically, if he was too nice or too wonderful, I would have no interest. I'd kick myself for that later on in life, but the truth is, had I attempted that I would have squandered it anyway.

If you don't heal the trauma brought about from your family of origin, you are doomed to repeat it. And, boy, did I wish I knew that beforehand. But, honestly, if someone had told me that or warned me, would I have even listened? If my cousin had told my mom that my dad was unfaithful—in an incestual way, no less—before they had married, would she have left him? Probably not.

I was so certain that the conviction of not wanting to be like my parents was enough. Also, I was so sure that love was enough to keep a relationship together—I mean no one taught me any different. And I was absolutely one hundred percent positive that I was the picture-perfect dating partner, girlfriend, and later mother, fiancée, and wife. But in reality, I would just move from one toxic relationship and family system to another. Even though in a way it was by default (like a program I was running), what I created was very much of my own doing or not doing and my inability to see what was really happening.

Even if we know something logically (like what we want in a partner), we still attract or gravitate to the familiar. Not only attract but unconsciously co-create. A very wise therapist told me, what felt like years too late, that I would emotionally break down any man who I was in a relationship with until I could utter the words, "See, you are just like my father!" And in many ways, he was right. I grew up believing that I was a worthless nothing. I felt unloved, unheard, and unseen. I had no voice and no identity. This flower could hardly blossom.

Craving Love

I remember longing for love as far back as I can remember. My first boyfriend was in the third grade and by fifth grade my new beau and I had already made plans of getting married. Not that there's inherent dysfunction in that, by any means. In fact it's quite natural. But I remember it being something that I truly *longed* for. At first boyfriends meant just that—saying you had a boyfriend. I wouldn't actually hold hands with or kiss a boy until I was thirteen. As I got older, of course, exchanges with boys became more physical. Out of all the boys I came across I remember this amazing guy—he was a little older. He was a friend of a friend and we hooked up while I was on vacation visiting her. He actually seemed interested in my pleasure and his only intention was to make me feel good. That felt like a big contrast and very positive to me. Most of the other boys you could tell were really in it just to say they had or just to get themselves off or just something they felt they needed to do or *had* to happen. Those exchanges didn't go too well with me. I made them feel so horrible to even attempt touching me in a sexual way.

These poor guys had no idea how broken I was, and neither did I really.

I remember often feeling obligated to partake in sexual experiences. In certain instances, I didn't know how to say no. It would not be until after marriage and divorce that I could actually embrace my sexuality and sex as a tool for my own pleasure and a beautiful and powerful way to truly connect to someone and express love. A mutual exchange. Imagine that?

A Magnet for Unwanted Attention

I also felt like a magnet to all unwanted male/sexual attention and predatory and pervertedness behavior in general. Incest even. I remember as far back as elementary school being followed by a man in a white van and thankfully learning if you are ever being followed to walk in the opposite direction that traffic can flow. Luckily, it was a one-way street and so I did just that. In junior high school, there was a man who lived near my school who would stand in his second-floor window completely naked every day. How did I, of all people, notice this? Another time there was a man walking toward me near my home who was dressed in only a T-shirt—nothing else. The T-shirt that did not go down much further than his belly button. Ugh! And then that other guy in a car near my high school who was clearly masturbating as I walked by. What was it about me? This was more than your regular cat-calling, which also unfortunately seemed like the norm for a young girl. And while way too many women and girls experience this behavior, I believed I was in some bubble where all these things were happening only to me because I had the belief that it was all I was good for.

One incident really stood out as a moment where I could feel my body completely freeze up and detach. My three girlfriends and I were on the train heading to the beach early one summer morning. We had to change trains several times to get there from our neighborhood. The further away from our town we traveled, the more stops the train made and it seemed more people were getting off than on. Before we knew it, we were the only people on the train except for one man who sat directly across from us and he began masturbating. I couldn't believe what was happening. All we could do was just turn around to look out the window so our backs were toward him. I wish I had the courage to say something. I wish the conductor or another adult came in at that same moment but it didn't happen. Thankfully he got off at the next stop and I was grateful for once that I wasn't alone in it.

And lastly, if things couldn't get any worse, there was an older cousin on my mother's side. A first cousin. Although he was just a few years my senior, he was an adult and I was still a child. He began taking an interest in me. He wanted to teach me how to drive and show me around the area where he lived, which was in the suburbs—I lived in the city. He tried to convince me to lose my virginity to him and keep it "in the family" because this was a "normal" thing back in Sicily where our families were from. He was grooming me. One day I was over at his house for Thanksgiving. I was wearing a short plaid skirt. He was making comments about my body and why boys would like me, saying I was "thick." He asked me to take a drive to a nearby lake. What possessed me to go? I felt like my aunt knew something was off with him because she asked me not to leave and there was an uncomfortableness in her tone, like a warning. Again ignoring glaring signs and intuition, I went. While we were out, this cousin asked me what I would do if he tried to kiss me, and I told him I would slap him and that was the end of our friendship. Not surprisingly he would end up being fired from more than one position because of his inappropriate behavior with minors.

Adventures in Dating

I never really "dated." I kind of just accepted whatever came my way. I wasn't looking for anything in particular except the feeling of being really loved. I do remember this one summer, however; it was 1996 and I was just a few months shy of nineteen. I was having such a fun time exploring my male options. It was the closest to actual dating I ever really got. I honestly wish I had spent more time doing so. I would truly not "date" again until I was in my forties! Allowing yourself to be courted is such a good practice of seeing and understanding what you want and getting to know yourself in the process, but I was completely unaware of that at the time. I was talking to a different boy in almost every borough. One from Brooklyn, another from the Bronx. And one more who lived in Queens. His family owned a well-known funeral home in my community and I will never forget him inviting me over and making me shrimp scampi—the first meal any "boyfriend" had ever cooked for me. Thinking back, he would have been the sensible choice. He was romantic and his family was successful. Of course, we don't attract what we want or what's necessarily good; we attract what's familiar. As a result, I settled on the bad boy from Brooklyn. There's always been something about those Brooklyn boys that I loved. I actually went on to marry one. The funny thing is that I felt like I *had* to choose one boyfriend, instead of really finding what was right for me. I could have continued exploring and enjoying myself, but unconsciously I settled on what reminded me of the first relationship with a man I had.

On Love: Part One

I met Liam at Club Expo in New York City—he was most definitely high on drugs at the time, but the naive little me didn't know it. He was gorgeous, with washboard abs and the most beautiful green eyes. He lived exactly eleven miles away from me—exit 11 on the Belt Parkway. He worked at a driving range. Thinking back, I don't remember us really having very much in common. He took me to a few cool restaurants and famous eateries in his neighborhood that I will still frequent today, but I can't recall a real true deep connection. I don't really think I was capable of that. I pretty much kept people at arm's length expecting them to hurt me. If you recall, I was always waiting for the other shoe to drop. Every boy I met that summer was strikingly handsome in their own way. Deep down I didn't really believe I was deserving of someone who was good in any way even if it was just outward appearances. And, of course, the signs were there pretty early on that this person had wounds too and difficulty expressing his hurt in healthy ways, but I ignored them for a chance at "love." The other problem is that where there is constant fear, there can't be real vulnerability, but I couldn't see that back then either.

I remember early on in the relationship I paid for a cab one evening to go visit him at work. Not too long before I arrived, he was choking his ex-girlfriend in a car. Yes, he told me this very detail, and I officially made him my boyfriend anyway!

We moved quickly through the honeymoon phase and the relationship started showing signs of being completely unhealthy pretty early on—as if that wasn't a frightening enough sign. I don't really think it felt alarming because I thought to myself, "He would never do that to me!" Again, ignoring not even just intuition but pure logic.

It was during this period in my life that I began using cutting as an emotional escape to deal with the feelings this relationship was bringing up for me. Feelings of not being worthy of love. When you don't have the safety of love growing up, you always believe you will be abandoned. When you feel that way, you can't actually ever relax. And when you are, in addition to that, severely abused and mistreated, you can't possibly choose someone who will truly love and honor you—at least, that was the case for me. In fact, even if they did, you would find every reason to believe they didn't. I don't really blame anyone I ever dated for things turning out the way they did. I spent a lot of time uselessly blaming the men I would encounter, but the truth is you teach people how they can treat you and what they can get away with. It really is our job to have self-worth and boundaries and say hell no to the first sign of serious trouble. Not to say that two willing people can't work out erroneous relationship patterns, but you need awareness and a lot of hard work for that.

Ironically, my relationship with Liam ended with him choking me in my car almost two years later. Luckily, I had the sense to walk away immediately following that. It's sad that this was my first experience with what I thought was real love and intimacy. Liam was the man I was willing to kill myself over. I attempted to take my own life while dating him. But it really wasn't his fault; it was the deep feelings of unworthiness that the relationship brought up for me.

I drove to Liam's house to surprise him with chicken soup one night when he canceled plans because he was "sick." When I arrived, he and his best friend were checking themselves out in the mirror all dressed up and heading out to a club! This little incident crushed me. The incongruence between *I love you* and anything that was very unlike that—like his lying, for example—was something I could not handle. This pointed to a deep dark wound, but it wouldn't be opened up again and ready to heal until much, much later. Luckily my attempt at ending my life failed, and it turns out you can't date the bad boy and lead a happy and successful life. In fact, he choked me because he was upset that the attempt didn't really affect me in the way it should have, and that he drove with his mom all the way from Brooklyn to Queens for nothing! The toxic cycles that we fell into became very disruptive in my life. Because of him and his incessant calling while I was at my job when we were arguing almost got me fired. I couldn't make it through my second semester of college because of all the chaos and I withdrew from all my classes. Eventually when I could not catch up and make up the work, those withdrawals all turned to Fs.

I later learned that he tried to commit suicide over a breakup with his previous girlfriend and when ours turned sour as well, his parents ordered him to rid his life of anything I ever gave him and stay away from me. They forced him to go no contact. I am so grateful they did because I am sure we would have cycled back into it again. Through social media, he and I caught up briefly years later, and I learned that he struggled with addiction most of his adult life and lost a lot of people he loved because of it. I don't blame him at all for the role he played in my life. I just wish I had the sense to see what the entire thing was revealing about me. Instead, I would cycle into something similar once again.

Like I said, the people in our lives mirror our internal landscape many times. The things they bring up in us are an invitation to heal those patterns. I grew up with chaos and because disorder felt comfortable and familiar it led me to keep recreating experiences that felt the same way. Unfortunately we can't always see the pattern and therefore end up repeating the same lesson until we do.

On Love: Part Two

My second serious relationship happened two years after meeting Liam. Another Brooklyn boy. Not as bad as the first; he was super sweet. Equally as gorgeous in a different way. He was tall, dark, and handsome. Such a gentleman, he asked permission before he kissed me for the first time. Nick knew he wanted me from day one. We met three years prior to officially dating at a birthday party (he had braces at the time and he was too shy to talk to me). We would go on to see each other again at an engagement party, but by then Liam was on my arm. The third time I saw him we were now at that same couple's wedding, and Liam was old news by then. I guess three times is a charm because I drove Nick home that night, and we began spending almost every day together from that point on.

Things were going great, at first. He wasn't into playing games and he made it clear that he liked me and his actions backed that up. He was consistent. This felt good to me. He showed up and I never felt any pressure around the physical, although he certainly was really interested in what I did with the other boys that came before him. He had a lot of old-fashioned views around sex and intimacy, which didn't feel like a bad thing. But it was more than that, he made me feel bad about any prior experiences with boys. He needed to know the details of previous partners. I'm not sure if this came from insecurity on his end or just from that very traditional point of view. All I did know is that it reinforced the feelings I had around the idea that anything sexual is bad, that's all that I am good for, and I am just a bad person, period.

Despite this, I translated the first few months as "going well"—at least I thought they were—but in hindsight part of me only felt secure because I felt like I had the upper hand or control in the situation. Meaning, I kept him at arm's length, never really letting him in completely, subconsciously protecting myself from being hurt. Nevertheless, we kept moving forward and eventually he introduced me to his family. At first, I felt lovingly embraced by them. This felt so good because being part of a family was another thing I desperately longed for. However, the more I was in it, the more I realized it wasn't really quite what it seemed. Although things didn't feel right, I felt like I could not break free of it, I was already in too deep somehow. The warning signs were all there. I chose to ignore them like I did so many times before.

Much like my own family, you were only welcome if you complied like a "good girl." You were not allowed to have a voice. You were not allowed to have a difference of opinion. You were not allowed to speak the truth. How dare you say something, how dare you stand up for yourself? Who are you to call out bad behavior and think anyone will listen? You are an outsider and you will always be—that's what the experience felt like for me. There was a lot of groupthink going on, and going against the hive mentality was a big no, no. It's interesting because on the day I finally met Nick's mother and sister, Nick's brother's wife hinted at the fact that this family was one to run far away from. This was now September (six months into the relationship). Unbeknownst to me at the time, Nick secretly was dreading this day, because apparently his sister created friction with any female who entered the family unit by way of her brothers. Little did I know with her help, Nick and I would create similar family patterns to the ones I grew up with: triangulation, gaslighting, etc.

I don't remember his sister-in-law's exact words, but it was a warning to stay away. She said it jokingly of course, but I didn't find out until too late that there was truth in her statement. I was in love with Nick. I loved the way he showed up consistently for me and completely. His dependability made me feel so safe. There was not a thing this man wouldn't do for me; at least, it seemed this was true in the beginning. I didn't realize that long before he and I ever met, he had fractured himself into tiny little pieces to be the consistency for everyone: his mother, his father, his sister, his brothers, his friends—all while putting himself last. And there was one friend in particular, his best friend, that relied on him in a way no healthy friend should. There was codependency everywhere, but once again, I was in no position to understand any of it nor see it at the time.

The night we officially started seeing each other was March 6, 1998—the night of the wedding. He sweetly ditched his ride (without telling the person) for me when I offered to drive him home. Nick gave me his jacket when I was cold, tipped the valet for me—he didn't even have his driver's license yet! And at the end of the night, he asked if he could kiss me goodbye. No one had ever asked me permission for anything. It was incredibly sweet, romantic, and a new concept to me. I felt on top of the world. I felt chosen and claimed, but the idea would quickly go on to terrify me. I never understood why he was so sure, so certain about us, but I would soon find out that his loyalty to his family would always come first. And through it all, I would be continuously reliving unconscious patterns.

Even if these experiences were not true (meaning not actually happening), my mind would have me believing it so I could prove the erroneous beliefs I had about myself to myself. Does that make sense? Even if something is not happening, you will make it so that you can prove yourself unlovable, unworthy, and so on or you will choose partners who you can mirror the dynamic with.

Did I really realize I grew up with a toxic relationship with the masculine? No. Could I have ever really had a chance without addressing the abuse? Definitely not. What were the chances I'd attract a healthy male? Slim to none. Was I truly capable of trusting and loving a man fully after what my father had done to me? Another no. Heck, I didn't even know what to do with kindness from a man! I undermined every sweet thing he tried to do, like the time he bought me a dozen yellow roses and had them delivered to my job—just because. I got mad at him!

I subconsciously knew I sure as hell was never going to let a man control me. A large part of me always knew that, so I found a man I could try to control. Of course, love is not at all about control, but all relationships with men felt that way to me and I didn't understand it at the time. It was all a jumbled mess in my mind. I didn't realize what true protection felt like. What masculine provision felt like. So, I pushed back as much as I could.

The true and utter joy that a man can add to a woman's life? I was not aware of it. I did not have a dad to look up to. I did not have a male role model to guide or teach me. No one really took an interest in me in a positive way. I did have one major male influence who used, abused, manipulated, and exploited me. I had no fighting chance.

My Body Shutting Down

My body appeared to be betraying me right around the time Nick and I became "official." I was twenty years old and he was just seventeen days shy of nineteen when we started dating and by now we'd known each other for about seven months. While I felt like he was a dream come true, I believe his intense love, dominating nature, and masculine traits (the way he claimed me from day one), all scared the ever-loving shit out of me. He knew that he wanted me, and I very much wanted to follow and trust his lead because he showed up for me in a way no one ever had. He was consistent; he was every single thing that my family wasn't. His love reminded me of aspects of Nonna's love (at least it did in the beginning).

He took on the role of truly being my everything. My friend. My lover. My family. And I put so much pressure on him to be just that. To fulfill all of my needs because he fulfilled so many of them without me asking that I just really thought that he could fill the deep, deep void that I subconsciously knew was there but didn't completely comprehend.

My plan was always to leave my parents' home as soon as I could. Nick was such a big help in setting up my new place when I finally made the transition, and I set boundaries for the first time in my life. The physical distance helped, and I told my mother that my father was not welcome. This was a huge deal. She blamed my roommate, my best friend at the time, because leaving as a single woman was so shameful for a traditional Italian family; however, I asked her to please look in the mirror when searching for a person to place fault.

Nick and I started dating in March, I was moved out by June, and what felt like overnight my body started shutting down. The more Nick loved me, the more frightened I became. I continued to keep him at arm's length. I continued to see other men and would tell him about it too. I introduced him as my "friend" until the day I could not contain my feelings.

On October 2, 1998, the words *I love you* just came tumbling out of my mouth during an emotional exchange and so then there was no going back, and we became "official." We were no longer just dating; we became an "item"—again, it was by default with no actual conscious choice on my part. Now I wish I would've seen the red flags in my fear, because my fears would later go on to devastate this relationship in an irreparable way. And this person who, like me, only ever wanted someone to love them, would be shattered by his very first deep connection with a woman.

We can talk more about how past trauma affects your relationships; however, when you're operating from unconscious trauma (the scared child within), you're in an entanglement, not a true relationship.

Nick started to spend many overnights with me, but I couldn't make the connection at the time between his love and me feeling that I was buried alive. I developed low grade fevers, a sore throat, and just an overall feeling of being sick and weak constantly. I had zero energy. Holding my arms up to blow dry my hair was too hard for me. I slept a lot. Taking a shower was a chore, and Nick jumped right into a caretaker role. At the time it made me love him even more, but little did I realize we were slipping into codependency.

I sought out help from doctors. I was tested for Lupus, AIDS, and what felt like everything under the sun at the time to help me to find the cause of why I was feeling the way that I was. I even had a CT scan done on my brain! The feeling of fatigue overwhelmed me. It was as if a huge weight was pressing down on me, and I really could not understand just what was happening. Eventually, I was diagnosed with Chronic Fatigue Syndrome (CFS).

Stuck in Cycles

Nick chose me. I told you he did, but I found every reason to believe it wasn't enough. He wasn't enough. Why? Because I was not enough. But at the same time, I also felt like I said yes a lot to whatever came my way. I was so desperate for love and a husband like my mother told me I needed to have; however, I had no actual standards. I had no measuring stick to which to compare these suitors too. If I had grown up in a safe loving home, would I have chosen him? Maybe I still would have, I don't know. But it would have been with better boundaries, that's for sure. And maybe we would not have created the mess we made. We will never know.

I didn't set boundaries in our relationship and neither did he. The outside forces of our two-person family, turned three-person family, turned four-person family unit never stood a chance from all that external pressure.

Nick had a sister who was more like a mother to him. Both the product of a family affected by trauma as well. The couple divorced when Nick was ten. The youngest and surprise baby of his parents, Nick was an only child in many ways. All of his siblings were adults by the time his parents split and he, still a child, was left to handle many adult matters alone. Sound familiar? After the divorce, his mother wasn't around as much. So, this older and only sister took on the role of his mother in many ways. She too was the golden child in some sense, at least to their mom. She was also the child everyone was afraid of/ covered up for because they would rather ignore her dysfunction than deal with her displeasure.

She created a very inappropriate bond with her brother in that she saw herself as the most important woman in his life. Expected him to always rely, confide, and consult with her. You can imagine why my other future sister-in-law was warning me. Nick's sister found reasons to criticize and undermine any woman that threatened her relationships with her brothers and in her eyes invaded her family dynamic. But as the woman to date her pride and joy—I had much more to deal with. Years later she stated that she felt as if I was competing with her, which goes to show you how she viewed their relationship in her mind. Why would I need to compete with my sister-in-law over the affection of my husband? It really made no logical sense; however, there was no way I could unravel that from my disempowered state of mind.

It also felt like triangulation all over again. She was like a puppet holding the strings and communicated her disapproval of me to others—through Nick, through his mother—but rarely if ever directly to me.

In fact, all this animosity began one day when I realized she wasn't speaking to me, but both his mother and Nick said I was imagining it. No argument had occurred between the two of us so I had no idea what was going on. When I wanted to confront her about it, Nick and his mother tried to dissuade me. Apparently she was someone not to be questioned—especially if she was angry or upset. So here I was in another situation where my reality was being denied (gaslighting) and I was being silenced in order to avoid "rocking the boat." The other big issue was that any time Nick and I had a problem, he went to her for advice. While he was intent on working through things, she appeared intent on compiling evidence as to why I was no good. His aim was to move through issues, and hers was to hold on to them and hold them against me. I had no idea that this was going on behind my back but this was clearly a recipe for disaster.

A Medical Diagnosis

CFS was a rabbit hole of unanswered questions within itself, as it is a diagnosis based on checklists and a process of elimination. It was basically a diagnosis of "I don't know what else it could be, so let's call it this." In my unrelenting pursuit to find an explanation, I enrolled in a study at a VA (Veterans Affairs) hospital for people diagnosed with Gulf War Syndrome since it was so similar. A young doctor or psychologist—I don't know his title nor do I know his name, but I wish I could thank him today—asked me if I had ever had anything traumatic happen to me. I paused for a second and then said, "Ummm, actually, yes." He introduced me to four letters that (although I never really wanted to be defined by) helped me to understand this mind and body connection even more. Those letters were PTSD, the acronym for post-traumatic stress disorder. He felt that my physical symptoms were a result of a past trauma. How could that be? How could trauma from so, so long ago manifest itself into the symptoms of being physically sick with a fever, a sore throat that never went away, and a feeling of malaise that had taken over my life? This was a big eye opener for me, the idea that unresolved trauma can cause physical symptoms and it's really not all in your head!

I truly believe that my relationship with Nick opened the floodgates of something that I had been burying for so long. There was something about our relationship that triggered my pain even more deeply than Liam ever could, and I still don't know what it was specifically. Was it our intimate relationship? He wasn't the first person I had ever been intimate with, but there was something about him, something about the relationship (and not anything that he did wrong) that brought up all of my trauma. I don't know if it was because he was tall and had dark features like my father. I don't know if it was because he was so one hundred percent sure that he wanted me and wanted to claim me as his own that scared me. I don't know if it was the deep feelings I had for him that made me want to hightail it in the opposite direction. As I said, I know part of it had to do with never wanting to be controlled by a man ever again, but it also may have had to do with our own erroneous views around sex too. I wasn't sure but my body was responding.

Regardless of the reason, I would remain oblivious to the relationship connection as a trigger for quite some time. The PTSD realization led to my first experience with Cognitive Behavioral Therapy (or talk therapy) because that was the only modality I really saw as a solution back then. My dad had a psychiatrist and my brother did too—ironically my brother's panic attacks started when he was seventeen. Here, at a similar age, my body was sending me loud and clear messages that something was wrong, yet in a very different way.

Early Stages of Healing

I sought out a psychologist instead, as medication was a big no-no for me. Talk therapy was the only "mental health" healing modality I had ever really heard of, although I would later learn that there are infinite pathways to healing. I would also learn that most mental health issues are caused from unprocessed emotions and you guessed it, trauma! My father was on medication for most of my life, and I in no shape or form wanted to resemble him. For most of my life he was really a shell of a person with no drive or ambition. Therefore, I looked at it as a bad thing even though I now know it can be necessary and even life saving in certain situations.

Not too long after I began therapy (I don't even remember how I found this woman), I invited my mother to participate in a session with me. I wanted so desperately for her to finally care about the pain that I was in. I wanted her to validate and acknowledge my experiences. In that forty-five minutes or an hour, I shared with my mother why I felt so hurt by her inactions when it came to protecting me from my father. She cried what felt like a lot of fake tears. She still felt very disconnected from me and anything I went through and the exchange did nothing for our relationship. I couldn't connect with her pain and she could not connect with mine. It felt insincere. In fact, it felt like none of it was helping. Session after session felt pointless with the therapist. I talked and she listened and I felt like we never got anywhere. At the time, I didn't understand the purpose of it because it did not seem to be helping. This just goes to show you that not everyone is good at their profession and/or that one method may not work for everyone. This particular therapist felt unqualified and/or ineffective to me at the time and because of my experience with her, I didn't return to traditional talk therapy until my marriage was already on the brink of divorce, some ten years later.

So, after trying therapy, with what felt like no luck, I did what I always did to survive—I kept busy. I did every single thing except look at the actual thing that was eating away at my soul. I was a super high achiever. Because of my mother's life experiences, she taught me never to depend on a man. So, I didn't. My mother's highest expectations of my life were for me to be a bank teller, because, to her (due to her upbringing), getting to wear nice clothes and work in an air-conditioned space meant you had made it. Luckily, I had the drive to dream bigger. Through an amazing program at my high school for seniors that I was asked to participate in because I had almost all the credits I needed to graduate, I was offered a job at JP Morgan. So in that last year of high school I would alternate between school and corporate America week after week.

At the young age of seventeen, my mother shunned the idea of me going to college. She thought it was a waste of money because in her eyes I had achieved success after JP Morgan offered me a full time job upon graduation, but luckily I didn't listen. Refusing to help me, I paid for every single cent (except for the one semester I begged my father to give me money for tuition—which he immediately asked to be repaid) of both undergraduate and graduate school. I had no choice but to work full time during the day and go to school at night while simultaneously incurring student loan debt.

The feeling of my body shutting down, though, never really resolved itself. Eventually I got fired from my job, so I made the painful decision to move back home to focus on college full time. I justified this by converting the basement of our family home into my own separate apartment (fully financed by me) protected by walls as well as lock and key. And although it took me 7 years just to get that first degree, it was worth it. It felt good to actually set a goal, go after it, and achieve something big for what felt like the first time in my life.

This also was the beginning of me being introduced to the relationship between nutrition and the presence of disease in the body. As well as understanding the mind-body connection. I read this incredible book called *The Cure for All Diseases*,[2] which got me into juicing fresh fruits and vegetables. Although I didn't stick with it at the time, I would later find my way back to the mind-body health connection once again.

Death, Rebirth, and a Calling

It was around this time my relationship with Nick began to fall apart. Plagued by the same cycles and patterns of both feeling unheard and not truly loved, we broke up in September of 2001. Nick however did not give up, he was relentless in pursuing me and although so many of the ways he used to get me back in hindsight were so unhealthy, it felt like love to me. We got back together on February 3, 2002, and exactly six days later I lost the most important person in my life—Nonna. Ninety-two years, nine months exactly—three months shy of her ninety-third birthday, she left this earth.

---

2. Hulda Rehehr Clark, *The Cure for All Diseases* (New Century Press, 1995).

Nonna Caterina was my namesake and my mama in so many ways. Her love healed and touched places I still can't fully comprehend. The older she got, the more I gave thanks every night before I closed my eyes for one more day with her.

When my mother was little, Nonna was very sick and they didn't think she would make it. I am so glad she did because I don't know where I would have been had it not been for her big and all-encompassing love.

The last time I saw Nonna, she was all alone in a hospital room. I remember being so frightened for her because she wouldn't have any way to communicate due to the language barrier. Before I left that evening, I made sure to teach her to use the call button if she needed assistance, but I thought: "How terrible to not be able to speak the language, communicate, share your needs, speak your truth."

Nick was with me that night. We told Nonna that we had decided we were going to get married (we weren't engaged, but we had just made that declaration of love to each other following the recent breakup and reconciliation). I told her we wanted her at our wedding. She said: "Si dio vuole" (if God wants). I guess God didn't want because her spirit transitioned on February 9, the very next day, before I got the chance to see her again.

And I often wonder—did she leave the role of protector to my boyfriend? She said she couldn't leave until she knew I was okay. Did our declaration of marriage make her feel that it was okay to leave me now? It was the exact thought that entered my mind at the exact moment of her death, and intuitively I felt it as truth. Although I went through so much of life feeling like I was in a fog, things pertaining to nonna always felt crystal clear even when she was no longer physically with me.

I selfishly would have hung on to Nonna forever, but I knew that wasn't what she wanted. She spoke of death often, never with fear, but with absolute certainty of the next life waiting for her, and I believed her. She wanted to be reunited with her husband, my Nonno, who she had lost thirteen years prior. I knew she was right, and I would go on to have my own experiences with communication from the other side in the years to follow, and by Nonna herself.

Nonna wanted to be buried in blue. She spoke of this often, driven by her connection to Mother Mary and the fact that she was always draped in blue. Although Nonna physically was gone, her lessons continued and continue to impact me. The lesson of communication she left behind, among many, was a powerful one.

Nonna refused to give up her home, even though each of her children offered that she come live with them. She was fiercely independent and made it clear that the moment she wasn't, she would leave this earth. She would often fall in her apartment. The last time she did, she ended up in that hospital. Nonna was told she needed to go to rehabilitation to relearn to walk. They felt she was too old for surgery, and her heart would not survive the anesthesia.

She had told my mother in the hospital that she would never get out of the bed again and that she would never walk again. She was right. Her words had power. She never made it to the rehabilitation center.

I was planning to take my mom to visit her the day she passed. To bring her some clothes. I went to the mall with a friend in the morning, and my mom was working in the garden. We were planning to go together later on. While I was at the mall, my friend and I took a break to eat, and I felt this wave of sadness come over me, and I started to cry but didn't know why.

I got the call that Nonna died while I was in the middle of Macy's and the world stood still. I had told Nonna I was getting married. She knew someone else would take the role of caring for me. And she could no longer be independent, and she wanted no part of that.

I was completely devastated and heartbroken, but I also was happy for her because she got what she wanted. She went into cardiac arrest and was successfully revived, only Nonna immediately left again. She knew what she wanted and knew what she did not. No manmade thing was going to change that.

Our connection feels so divine in so many ways because I know she was here in part to make sure I made it, that my light could see its way through the darkness. She was that mirror and reflection for all the goodness in me. There's so much I would ask her if she were still here. Like did she have moments of fear where she didn't feel so in control of her life and her destiny? Did she know for sure life was not over even though it may have seemed that way? Ironically I would go on to have moments like that and I wish I had her there to talk to.

As I mentioned before, the older Nonna got, the more I thanked God every night for one more day with her because I knew how lucky I was to have her in my life for so long. I knew she wouldn't be here forever, yet she lives through me still. She's the reason I strive to be the light for others. In that way, her love will last forever.

It's been eighteen years and I still feel all the pain of that day. I miss Nonna so much, but her love carries me through the hard times, even now. Death is such a great reminder that love transcends all things and that no greater power exists. One day I know I will hug her again, but for now I have so much work to do to continue what she taught me. I am so grateful to her for showing me what real love is and the power it holds to transform the darkest of realities. This too reminds me of the life cycle of the butterfly. No matter how scary the process may be, it is necessary for the caterpillar to break down to become the butterfly in order for the future super generation to become a reality. I like to think Nonna fought her way out of a life-and-death situation for the realization of not only me but for my future butterflies as well.

I wrote the story of when I last saw Nonna in my post-graduate essay to get into one of the most competitive speech-language pathology programs in New York City. The theme? The importance of using your voice to communicate. Of course, at the time it was a literal translation. Whether it was learning a new language or overcoming a language disorder, the meaning was similar. However, over time that theme of helping others find their voice has taken on greater significance in my life. I feel called to not only help women and girls find their voice in a literal way but in a deeper, more profound way. A greater mission was revealing itself but the bigger picture wasn't quite clear yet.

The Birthing of a Super Generation

Nonna did something else before she left me. She gifted me with a baby girl. Before she passed, before even falling and being hospital-bound, she told me to have a baby and name her after her. I guess she was certain I'd have a daughter. I told her she was crazy. I said (in Italian): "Nonna, I'm not even married!"

After she passed, I knew immediately that someone would get pregnant. My first thought was my sister-in-law (my brother's wife)—I was certain it would be her, since she and my brother were actively trying to have a baby. Little did I know it would be me. Embedded in here was another display of Nonna's lessons. Nonna continuously taught me how powerful words can be and how intention can be spoken into existence and that what is meant to be will always find a way. Two weeks after Nonna's wake, I conceived the most perfect baby girl who does indeed carry on the Caterina name. When I gave birth to my first piece of absolute perfection, they wheeled us into recovery room 509. Nonna's birthday is May 9, 1909, and that was just one of the many signs of confirmation I received that she was there with me.

When I first found out I was pregnant, all the negative ways (for example, cutting myself) I had used to cope with my buried pain had to come to an utter and complete stop, and they did. However, I didn't realize stopping the self-harm was in a way keeping the pain trapped inside because I no longer had an outlet to get it out (no matter how dangerous my methods were). I was going to become a mother without any way to process this pain. So, in my quest to be the best mother and to set the best example, I unconsciously buried my pain once again.

When you look at every event in your life, every encounter, and every single body reaction with new eyes, you realize that almost everything is always leading you to healing or giving you a clue that something is off (in my case, way off). That GPS you come equipped with is always looking for equilibrium, the balance. Your body has every ability to heal and is always speaking to you. In one way or another, you are *always* on a healing journey (even with all the starts and stops), you just don't realize it. Sometimes we can't see it or refuse to until the signs are too loud to ignore and trust me that *will* happen.

I will forever be grateful for the gift of my daughter. What Nonna wants, Nonna gets, it seems. She truly lived life on her own terms. She knew how much power her words had to bring her desires to fruition. Remember, Nonna was supposed to be transferred to a rehabilitation center after her hospital stay and she told my mother she would never walk again even though she would be going to rehab for that very reason. However, Nonna had told me long before that she never wanted to be dependent on anyone and she meant it.

She taught me so much just about who she was and how she lived. I wish so much that she could have held not one, but both of her great-granddaughters, but Nonna and God had other plans. Life has plans that sometimes we will never understand and maybe we're not supposed to.

I wouldn't know how much her presence in my life shaped me until much, much later. Even writing her story in these pages has brought me many new realizations. Nonna changed my life. She saved my life. The simple act of her loving me so genuinely and purely allowed me to hold on to my light because in every instant she reflected it back to me. In the way she consistently showed up taught me that I mattered. Who has shown up as an angel in your life? Who can you thank for keeping you connected to that spark? If this person is still here in your life, send them a note of thanks.

Nick and I were five years into our relationship by now, and we were having a child together, almost two years after that we got married. In the "wrong" order, of course, because when did I do anything right? And there were no shortages of people telling us how much we fucked up, believe me. I had such high hopes for my marriage, even though, deep down, going in I knew it wasn't the right thing to do. I loved him. God, did I love him—or did I? It sure felt like love. But was it love? Was it the trauma, the familiarity that felt so good? Man, I drove that poor man crazy because I couldn't even discern what the fuck I was feeling! Life very much felt like it was happening to me. It felt like I had no control over it.

Despite all the confusion, I wanted so much for my daughter, our daughter. When she was conceived, it seemed as if nothing positive was going on. Nick was out of a job. I was a full-time student living in my parents' basement. He was still living at home with his mother and sister who wanted no part of us becoming a new and separate family. He was twenty-two about to be twenty-three, and I was twenty-four turning twenty-five right before birthing my first Queen. And whether that seemed young to some or not,—we had no business having a baby and becoming parents just yet; however, that was just what we were about to embark on. We were jobless and with no real home of our own, but somehow none of that felt like a deterrent for me.

I was so damn ambitious. I still am. I never let anything stop me. I was a fighter. I always have been. Nothing felt hard or impossible for me. It was almost as if the trials in my life were a given and because of them I just happened to learn how to function best under pressure. A result of the trauma and chaos, I imagine. Because of it, nothing scared me, but I would later see that fear over big things is normal—and I didn't feel them really because I spent so much of my life being utterly detached from myself.

Being constantly in chaos somehow prevented me from seeing the true gravity of the situation. Baby on the way? Living in a basement with no real income? No problem! Everyone around me seemed to be falling apart, but not me. I was over the moon with joy!

Nick began going out drinking every night. He couldn't handle the fact that he was going to be a father—a path that he intentionally chose, he would later explain to me. He told me he knew that he wanted me to be the mother of his children from the moment he met me. In hindsight, maybe he was seeing the present situation for what it really was, and maybe that was the first sign that he was not ready to take on that responsibility or just that he was responding to an actual BIG thing! But it didn't matter. Our baby was coming, whether he liked it or not.

Everyone else was coming apart at the seams, too! My mother, his mother, my brother . . . and his sister—oof, forget about it. Talk about overbearing, controlling, and operating from crazy fear. His sister was not having it! Not having her little brother achieve the things she never did before her and ironically never would.

In hindsight, I realized that I spent so much time looking for other people's approval and validation for my life that I never really stopped to realize they were *not* showing up in the ways I wanted to model my life after. I didn't realize that was what Nick was doing too. He wanted his family's approval so badly. Unfortunately, they were no gold standard for what we should have been measuring our lives against. I was surrounded by dysfunction, pleading for approval from people who were essentially operating from the very patterns I wanted to desperately break away from. It's almost funny now how naive I was. But despite that, I had the highest of hopes for our baby girl. I was full steam ahead, bursting with delight. While others were asking me whether I was keeping her, I was already dreaming up names for her and all the adventures we would have together.

I knew nothing would prevent me from achieving my dreams. Now I had someone to come along with me for the ride! How incredible would that be? Someone who would always love me. I mean truly *love* me. And that in itself was a lot of pressure to put on my growing little bean, but I was so hopeful. This baby was going to fill every gaping hole in my heart. And as for my babies, they were going to feel all the love that I never did. It would be a win-win, and I was gonna do it so much better than my parents or his parents did!

Of course, getting to experience the feeling of pure love is the wrong reason to have a child, but since she was coming anyway, I figured I would have the blessing of getting to experience a love like I had never known. And I surely did.

Our daughter came into this world with little celebration around her. Everyone was pretty much appalled at the fact that we were not married, but I had enough excitement in my heart for her arrival to make up for their lackluster reactions. I had a lot of experience being shitted on, and so none of this was anything different. Of course, it would have been nice, but there was a big part of me that never felt I deserved anything better anyway.

And although we didn't have her gender revealed—we wanted to be surprised—I knew for certain that Nonna's words were true. My first Queen came into this world during a nor'easter and a meteor shower. She was a powerful quiet storm. At birth, she didn't cry—she was so peaceful. She represented everything that was good and right in the world, in my world—for once in my life.

Eventually Nick got a job at a prominent New York City hospital, and it wasn't too long before he got me a job there as well. I worked as a physician office assistant for one of the leading Sarcoma specialists. Despite our troubled relationship, we really did beat some of the odds in big ways. We actually worked really well together achieving goals that we set out on. We went from being pregnant living in a basement with no jobs or income to purchasing a beautiful house on Long Island that we had professionally painted. We bought all new furnishings, I acquired my first college degree, we both secured great jobs, and executed a big Italian wedding all before our little girl turned two. And for that auspicious occasion, we celebrated with a real live pony party! To me it felt like the epitome of living the dream of having a big house in the suburbs. On the outside, it seemed we had it all aside from the white picket fence but the inside was a vastly different story.

Life on Autopilot

I didn't even dream of the future or set goals really. I was on autopilot—doing the things you're *supposed* to do. Find an Italian man, get married, and have babies. If I needed a job—I just got one. There was no time to worry, really. If I had a problem, I would find a way to solve it.

When the two of us first moved in together, it was in the apartment I made in my parents' basement, and when our little girl was almost twenty-three months old, we got married.

At one point I was going to graduate school, planning a wedding, buying a house, and raising a toddler. No problem. We bought the blue house on the corner with all the bedrooms upstairs, the way he wanted. The blue reminded me of

Nonna and her connection to Our Lady, and so I knew it was meant for me.

When we were having our home painted, I requested our daughter's room to be two shades of pink. Dark on the bottom half and light on the top. The first time she saw it, she looked around, took it all in, and said, "I love it, Mom, but can we make it blue?" I was always being reminded that Nonna was with me and her spirit came through big time in my beautiful green-eyed, curly haired little girl.

And here is where the butterflies really started showing up for me—or perhaps where I really began to notice. You know how people traditionally release doves on their wedding day? Well, I was called to release monarch butterflies, and I wasn't really sure why. Although I personally did not fully understand the level of commitment I was making at the time, a wedding is clearly a huge example of a major transformational period in one's life and can even be considered a rebirth of sorts. It's so interesting to me that I would be drawn to the monarch butterfly, even then (over eighteen years ago)!

To help you understand how unconscious I was and so clearly not out of the dysfunction I was—I let my father walk me down the aisle at my wedding. Both my parents actually! I desperately wanted this view of an ideal family—the fake image that they tried to sell me on. And I went on with the facade.

Nick and I got married in a church—the way *his* mom wanted. We were both so used to living for others and pleasing them that we couldn't comprehend how un-autonomous individuals we had become. We both lived from this program our family inherited, and we took it into our relationship. Do as the family says (group think) and everything will be okay.

In his family, his sister was the council. If she wasn't happy, she made sure everyone would know it. We both tried so hard to constantly put out the fires, keep the peace, and cover up the shame and the truth that it was inevitable that we would inevitably combust.

Everything comes back to your birth family and your relationship with one or both of your parents (or lack thereof). Even their relationship with each other. And many times, since trauma is not talked about, it makes it even easier to repeat. That's why it's so important not to fear the darkness. Nothing good comes of covering things up, cowering in shame, or hiding abuse. This is one of the reasons why telling my story has been so healing in itself. But sometimes that's honestly all you know. Awareness is essential. Nick and I didn't have it yet, nor did we ever reach that place together.

Despite this, on the outside, like I said, it seemed we were pretty successful as a couple. We worked hard and we saved. We bought the beautiful house in the burbs—although no white picket fence, still by all means . . . impressive. We had the nicest house of all our older siblings combined—remember, Nick and I were both the babies in our respective families. We had the traditional Italian wedding, and the nice car with all the bells and whistles, leather interior memory seats, sunroof—you name it.

We wrestled with our demons privately because (for the most part), I honestly don't think we were conscious of them or that we brought so much of them to the table. Even if it seemed we were a team in some ways, deep down we definitely were not.

Our families (mainly his) always had a say in what we did, and Nick would always listen, especially to his sister. We worked well together but only to a certain extent. I didn't hear him, and he didn't hear me. If there was a problem in our relationship, he would go to his sister, and she always somehow took it out on me. It's as if she was jealous of me on many levels. At times he would come to me with thoughts he passed off as his own and other times he just kept them inside feeling he really could not come to me. His loyalty to her left him feeling like he had to choose. It's interesting because I had similar relationships with other women in my life growing up. My mother who was jealous of the attention my father gave me, and my aunt who seemed jealous of my relationship with her son and her husband. I seemed to be surrounded by unhealed people and this strange triangulation dynamic.

Nick and I created this way of relating to our marriage that was similar to my home life growing up. I had this idea that I had to be chosen the way I wished my mom had chosen me over my dad. I kept re-creating it. I couldn't set boundaries and neither could he. My boundaries were consistently violated in childhood, so what did I know about creating some of my own now?

Super Generation: Part Two

Although our marriage was on shaky ground, I longed for another child. Our daughter was always asking us why she was the only cousin with no sibling, and together she and I prayed for her to have a sister. Was it the right thing to do? It didn't matter. I wanted what I wanted. Nick and I struggled to get pregnant a second time. We lost two babies trying to conceive our second miracle, so again, little to no celebration for our second-born either. No matter what I did, it felt like I couldn't do anything right because I was always looking for external validation. Even from my husband. My love tank was so empty, and I wanted everyone else to fill it. Without Nonna's big love and constant validation, I felt empty. I didn't know how to give that to myself.

When I finally got pregnant with my youngest daughter—our second slice of perfection. I knew for certain she was who I was waiting for. No other spirit came through because she was the one who was without a doubt meant to be.

At the time I was about to embark on a new journey as a newly licensed speech-language pathologist. I was one year into postgraduate school and working in various preschools across New York City. It seemed almost every class I was assigned to was doing a monarch butterfly release that year. I remember a monarch butterfly came to me as I was sitting on a Brooklyn stoop past sundown; it just circled near me. It felt truly surreal! Some of Nick's family members felt the butterflies were a sign from the girls' older cousin on their side who had recently passed away—I myself had never met her. Coincidentally (or not), my magical girl was born on the anniversary of this family member's death. I honored the connection by making my daughter's christening favors butterfly themed. One of them still remains clinging to a window in my home today.

Motherhood Heals

Even after all I had been through, I wanted so desperately to believe that I could have a normal family. In fact, I allowed my mother to watch our oldest daughter when I went back to work following my maternity leave. I specifically instructed my mother to keep my father away from my daughter. He was in no way allowed to be in my portion of the home. What made me think I could actually depend on her? Maybe it was wishful thinking, but years later I found out that she vehemently violated my trust. Not only that, but she also told me again my experiences did not happen and told my child, who was just a toddler, that her experiences did not happen! Events I witnessed with my own eyes! My mother was willing to allow the cycle of abuse to continue into the next generation. It was at that moment that it became exceptionally clear to me that the trauma ends with me. I had to learn this boundary thing the hard way. My daughter was no longer allowed in my mother's home. By now we were living on Long Island and I was driving my girl back to Queens for this unhealthy childcare, believe it or not. It ended that day. My mother had to be the one to drive to Long Island if she wanted to continue to be a caregiver, although I should have probably severed that tie too. We had no other help which is what I told myself, but I am sure there was a part of me who was scared to set that particular boundary. I kept my little one away from their home for many years after her birth as well.

My girls are perfect and the blessing in all of this. Children always are.

And I think there's a reason our kids are so different from each other and from ourselves. They are meant to teach us, guide us and help shine the light on our inner child that needs to heal. My firstborn was so easy. She came to me without trying and she never fussed. Her pregnancy was a joy; she was a reminder that I deserved to have happiness without pain. My second born, although I felt like I had to fight for her, taught me the power of what is meant to be. She also was just such an incredibly good baby. Neither one of them ever gave me issues with sleeping or eating or anything. They were just pure bliss to be around. People get tired of being pregnant or need breaks away from their kids. I never felt this way. They represented everything good in my life. All I wanted was to be the perfect mother to them. All I wanted was to create a family I didn't have for them. I felt like I failed in many ways, and it's difficult for me not to grieve the path I took, but I also know that any change may have resulted in me not knowing these two incredible humans, and I really wouldn't risk that for anything. We must not allow ourselves to get stuck in the cycle of what ifs. Trust that for some reason, good or bad, everything worked out as it should have and all of it helped to get you to where you are today.

Motherhood has challenged me in so many ways. My girls have shown me and continuously remind me who I want to be—as backwards as that may sound. They have been my absolute reason for healing, for wanting to get out of bed in the morning and to be better. Motherhood is a journey and a profound love like nothing I could have ever imagined. I am so beyond blessed. They have been my greatest teachers.

My girls are amazing manifesters too. They will set an intention and go after what they want. When my oldest was searching for the perfect high school, I truly didn't understand her choice. But she said, "Mom, you ever feel like you just know something?" Yes, baby girl, yes! She was reminding me of intuition. My youngest will say things, write them down or draw them, and they happen. When I try to create something in my life, she is my go-to. When it was her turn for high school, she made a list of what she wanted in school and that girl got every single thing she wished for!

I couldn't be prouder of them. They are fierce, powerful, sensitive, and so loving. At times they can get super quiet, but when they need to talk, they always come around. Nothing gets past them—they see and understand things that I don't even realize. They call me out when I am wrong, and I hear them. For that I know I have far surpassed the cards I was dealt. They have always known so much more than I have ever taught them, and they continue to make me proud knowing that they will soar far beyond what I have been or will be capable of. That has been my number one wish for them and they have already demonstrated that.

I really can't believe it sometimes but here we are. Two beautiful young powerful women, call me mom. How does it get better? I'm living and loving and waiting to find out.

And although I thought I was a great mom—I know I am a great mom—there were times when I struggled maintaining connections with them. I worried that if I held them too much, I would spoil them. What I would give to hold them even longer now! As they got older, if they wanted to hug me from behind, it startled me. But still this was medicine for me—the sign that I knew I had more work to do. I still catch myself disconnecting and dissociating at times but they always, always bring me back to the present.

Death, Destruction, and the Gifts They Bring

I suffered the profound loss of my Nonna right before I conceived our first child. Shortly after the birth of our second daughter, I lost someone else who was extremely special and close to me—my older cousin Mario. The oldest of my three cousins who lived next door to me. He really was more of a big brother figure in my life than anyone else. Mario died on his thirty-fifth birthday. And although his death started becoming imminent, the permanence of losing him threw me into a spiral. I had been numb most of my life and throughout my marriage, but leave it to death to really smack you awake. Grief and loss have a way of allowing you to get so crystal clear on what matters and what's not working. It really reminded me that life is so incredibly short, and I was determined not to waste any more time being unhappy.

When Mario died, everything came crashing down. I don't know if it was grief, a mid-life crisis, or just the shocking realities that death brings to the surface, especially when someone dies so young. Life is so incredibly short, and I realized that I wasn't really living. Mario's death taught me so much. It forced me to reevaluate my life and shine a light on the areas where things were really not working, namely my marriage.

Although today, Mario would have been forty-seven years old, for those of us who loved him—the world stood still on the day he turned thirty-five. I often think there must be some magic in leaving on the same day you entered the world. There must be some meaning behind it. I don't know. I think as humans we want to make something mean more than it is, but although his death made no sense, it all felt very special to me. And so many times, you really don't realize the impact that someone has made in your life, until there's a lot of space between you and those memories.

Mario was no stranger to growing up in a family where there wasn't a lot of love and affection displayed. Sometimes I chalk it up to a cultural thing. But is it really culture or just passing down trauma? Regardless of the reason, I always felt like it was so important to tell someone you loved them because I don't think you could ever say it too much if you truly meant it and we all really need to hear it.

Mario was diagnosed with a rare form of pediatric cancer called Ewings Sarcoma; it was even more rare that he had it as he was not a child at the time. It is a fast moving and aggressive cancer and unfortunately had already metastasized to his lungs when he was diagnosed—stage 4 right off the bat. I knew it wasn't good.

When Mario got sick, I was with him every step of the way. Nick and I had worked at the cancer hospital where he was being treated, and so we knew people and made things happen a little quicker, a little smoother. I went with him that first day to his appointment. He didn't like needles, but I held his hand and told him everything was going to be okay—even though deep down I was scared that it wasn't.

As time went on, I spent a lot more time with Mario, and I told him I loved him every chance that I could. At one point he remarked that it was nice—that I always made him feel so loved. That I said those things out loud.

Mario and I always had a special bond. Even though he was older, sometimes he would come to me for advice about girls and stuff. He was so super sweet. When he worked at the bank, I always took the time to visit him and when I left super early senior year for a ski trip, he was there to see me off and hug me when I got back. And the best was when he was already sick, he took a guy's trip and had to leave early for treatment but made it a point to visit me and the baby in the hospital shortly after I gave birth. There's so much I can tell you about him, but I would write forever.

Mario gave the best hugs. I think he and Nonna are the reason I love hugs so much. His presence really filled the room. He was so funny. He loved the color orange and penguins and Super Mario, of course. He loved Halloween and dressing up. The year he turned thirty-four, he threw the most fun Halloween, birthday, karaoke party—Mario was so full of life.

I miss him a lot too. I wonder what life would be like if he was still here. I wonder what the family would be like. I think: Would he have gotten married or had kids? He loved all of our kids.

It wasn't too long before he needed an oxygen tank every day, and eventually this landed him in the hospital connected to a machine that was doing the breathing for him.

On October 26, I woke up feeling so sad. I could not stop crying. Nick asked me what was wrong because I was on my way to see Mario with my brother. We had received the good news the previous day that Mario was breathing more on his own than the machine and that this was a good sign. I couldn't explain my sadness. When we got to the hospital our uncle told us that in the middle of the night Mario stopped breathing completely and now the machine was doing all the work. It was devastating, but it reminded me of the connection I felt when Nonna passed. It was the feeling that the end was coming for one of the purest hearts I knew.

The day we said goodbye, Mario did something really special for me. Although he couldn't speak because of the breathing tube and his hands were tied down so he couldn't rip it out, he somehow managed to get one hand free. He took my hand in his and brought it up to his face. Then, the best way he could, despite the medical apparatus in the way, he kissed it. It was his way of saying goodbye. I began to cry immediately. A single tear fell onto his nose, and I wiped it for him. Despite his limitations, he found a way to say goodbye to everyone in the room that day in his own unique way, but this felt so incredibly special to me. I feel like it was because of how open I was with my love for him that he could also be that way with me. That goodbye is a gift I will always treasure—thank you, Mario.

I told him over and over that it would be okay. That we would never forget him and Mario reminds me all the time that he's here. When you lose someone, you worry that there will be no new memories and the old ones will fade away, but Mario has a way of making new memories with us even though he is physically not here.

Like that first Christmas without him, I found a small metal penguin in the street outside his house over a light dusting of new fallen snow. I still have it in my car. And when I traveled across the country, I ended up at our older cousin Mario's house on his birthday! Or how that one year I went to a Halloween party and the first person I saw was dressed as Super Mario. He gave me his number that night. Nice try, cuz, but he was NOT for me!

I miss laughing with him, his silly faces, and sarcastic remarks. I miss coming to him for advice and vice versa. I will miss him for as long as I am here without him.

After he gave the okay (Mario gave the thumbs up), they disconnected him from the breathing machine—just his parents and brothers were with him. My brother and I and some friends were in the room next door. I heard my aunt's screams, and I knew he was gone but then the most beautiful thing happened. What felt like instantaneously, Mario's energy filled the room in the most expansive way. I felt him more in that moment than I had in the many days leading up to his death. It reminded me everything Nonna taught me that although death was an enormously painful transition for the living, it felt like a beautiful and freeing event for the departed. Mario felt exceptionally larger than life, no longer confined to a body incapable of allowing him to live as he wanted. It was a big reminder that death is not to be feared even though it is extremely difficult on the living who are left behind.

Pupa

Retreating into a Cocoon

The first time I told Nick I loved him, he responded with: "All I ever wanted was someone to love me." It was so profound—those words. Me too, Nick, me too. I was shocked. Honestly, I didn't think anyone else felt the same as I did, but I tucked it away, never asking him to elaborate. The words stuck with me. While I would revisit them much later on, he never did say why he felt that way. Maybe he felt invisible in a way I did. The youngest of four, eight years junior to his youngest sibling, perhaps he grew up feeling alone too. He was the only one to navigate his parents' divorce as a child; all the others were already adults. This had to have really shaped his life, but he was a good man. He really was. I like to think his intentions were good, as mine were. At the end of the day we were two well-intentioned very young adults who wanted to love and feel loved but our trauma got in the way. And we were without the tools to overcome it. Our demons danced together in a way that seemingly turned the dance floor into a bloody fucking mess.

I went from relationship to relationship thinking I had to pick one. Then, before you know it, I was becoming a mom and getting married, buying a house in the suburbs all by default. All because of someone else's ideas which turned into what I thought I *needed* to do. And don't get me wrong, I had to be a willing participant, but I never stopped to think if any of it made real sense. I even picked a career seemingly by accident. I was originally majoring in advertising and communications. I actually knew enough to understand I couldn't go into an industry that wasn't meaningful and when I realized a lot of advertising was psychological manipulation, I ended up taking up communication in a very different way. But believe it or not, becoming a speech language pathologist entered my sphere merely by flipping through a course catalog, landing on the page, and thinking, "hmm, this sounds good!" At the end of it all, I ended up with a husband, a career, two beautiful daughters, a blue cape on a corner property in a quiet residential neighborhood with a brand new SUV in the driveway but for some reason happiness eluded me.

And how could it not? I think deep down Nick and I never really trusted one another. I subconsciously feared men, and I felt in many ways due to his own experiences, he had a negative view of women. Our families really sucked in a lot of ways. It's like they were smiling to our faces while simultaneously expecting us to fail behind our backs. It was weird. It never felt good. I never felt truly supported from either side, and I am pretty sure he didn't either, but at the same time how could we know what that really felt like? My family was anything but loyal to me, and his family was almost overly loyal. Even if you were exhibiting bad behavior, they'd go along with it. Unless of course your behavior went against their rules, then they would abandon you too.

When the disconnect became too great for me to bear in the wake of Mario's death, against Nick's wishes, I filed for divorce. Unable to handle the deep pains in my marriage and the profound loss of Mario, I left him. I started dating as soon as I could, not realizing that leaving one person doesn't change your experience in relationships unless you yourself actually do the hard work to change the patterns. Again, it was unavoidable, and I inevitably repeated the familiar.

Although Nick and I were divorced—emotionally, spiritually, and physically–we were still very much enmeshed. We would continue to do this dance, him pursuing me, me pushing him away, and us becoming further and further trauma bonded. But I also believe a big part of it was we still had more lessons to learn from one another.

In between all this mess, there were other relationships we formed with others, but when all else failed, he was always there. We kept going back to each other until we were really forced by life to separate. That was such a hard lesson for me. If you don't end or amend toxic relationships for yourself, something will end it for you. Toxic relationships were killing me but they were familiar and all I knew. Consciously I knew I had to end the relationship with him for good, but I truly, truly did not know how. The fear of the unknown was far greater than the miserable pattern I was in.

Finding Beauty in Pain

It took me three years to understand the impact of my choice to devastate my family—that was how I came to view my divorce. While I did not obviously do this alone, I carried much of the guilt of feeling like I had failed our girls. The realization didn't come until Nick brought his girlfriend to the first day of school (a tradition we had previously reserved for the four of us despite both having significant others). Every year following our separation, Nick met me in front of the girls' school on their first day. I would take a picture of him with the girls and vice versa. On this day, however, I took a picture of my children, their father, and another woman in my place. Of course, I didn't say anything. I remained numb like I did to get through everything, even though it felt so upsetting, but he immediately called me as soon as I got home, apologizing, crying even. He said: "I love her, but it should be you."

We then left our respective partners and tried again. It would have been a beautiful story, only he ended up running back to her because nothing about me had changed. I wanted him, but I didn't want who he was and that was not fair to him. I was judgemental and controlling. Nevertheless, this crushed me. The man who loved me more than anything— the one I actually believed because he never abandoned me left me for someone else. It was a tough pill to swallow. It was a light shining on another gaping wound. Nick did, however, leave me with an enormous amount of wisdom among all the excruciating heartache. He told me he didn't think I was over what had happened to me as a child, and he felt it had affected our marriage. Of course, most people could rationally understand that; I mean, anyone with eyes could see that but, believe it or not, I really didn't see the true impact it made on me and all of my relationships until he said those words. This was a monumental moment in my life because I started gaining more awareness of the impact of my trauma. But I also took action, and that was key. That was so incredibly brave on my part. While it's easy to get caught up in should ofs and what ifs, it is important to acknowledge the work you have done.

I truly took to heart what Nick said, and I immediately poured into various books on the topic. The public library has been one of my greatest gifts. One of the books I took out was called *Stolen Tomorrows*. It was a book written for therapists to help treat women who were sexually abused as children. The book contained stories from real women. Although I was not a therapist, I was drawn to the title because I truly felt so much was stolen from me. I forced myself to read each and every story. I took in every detail, and I forced myself to be present with them. It was not comfortable, but from one story to the next, I saw myself in those pages.

Finally Feeling Validated

When I was done, I realized Nick was right. I sought out help. I looked at the back cover of the book, and it turned out the author was a New York City–based psychotherapist (I still lived just outside the city). He specialized in helping women who engaged in self-harm and were victims of childhood sexual abuse. He was trauma informed but specifically childhood sexual trauma informed (how sad that that really needs to be a thing). For the next eleven months, Steven became my therapist. This is a true testament to when the student is ready, the teacher appears.

Ironically, Steven was born the same year as my father, and it felt like he was brought into my life for so many reasons. He taught me that when you are a kid who is being abused in any way, you feel you have no choice but to blame yourself. In fact, as children, we don't perceive our parents as wrong or bad so instead we internalize it. And although it's something I didn't learn until this point, having already had two children and a failed marriage, it was so important for me to know and hear those words regardless of how late they seemed to have come. My therapist explained that, as children, we look to our parents for guidance, as role models. They're big people—they can't possibly be wrong. So, we turn that inward. Meaning if they are doing something to hurt me, then it must be me. It must be my fault. I didn't really have the conscious awareness of that thought process as a child, obviously, but Steven gave me such profound insight as well as a gift. It really felt like a Robin Williams, Matt Damon, "it's not your fault" moment.

It was after our second or third session that I had another huge realization. Steven had used the word *penis* during that particular session. He was explaining that subconsciously I knew that my father's penis was a weapon. It would not have mattered whether my father did anything with it or not, but at that moment in time that was how it was imprinted for me. This was a huge realization. It's not always about the trauma or the specific events of what happened. It has everything to do with how we internalize it and what we make it mean in that moment. Anytime my father had his penis out, it was a threat to me. I remember being so triggered by the word *penis*. I couldn't even listen to it. I had to ask Steven to stop. That night I had such a vivid dream, and the following morning I wrote to Steven. This was part of the email I sent:

It was with my dad and I confronted him about what he did to me, and in my dream, he accused me of sexually abusing HIM! Anyway, all I remember was hitting him very violently, over and over. I'm not sure if all that penis talk triggered this.

He responded with the following:

Yes, our last session provoked your dream. BUT the good news is that your unconscious is recognizing that you (in the character of your father) have identified the part of you that, as a child, only had yourself to blame. It's an important start and early in treatment to recognize this, on any level.

Holy shit balls! Wow! What an incredible revelation. It was so wonderful to receive this message. Steven made me feel validated in a way no one ever had. His wisdom and his presence in my life was so healing for me in many ways. It was one of the first experiences with a safe man I had, and on top of that, with someone who represented a father on some level.

We went on to work together for almost a year until I began feeling the pull to a more spiritual path, and our time together came to an end. Around this point, I also began a gratitude journal by way of an Oprah episode and learned about the power of positive affirmations from Louise Hay, both of which made a big impact on me. Eventually, they became huge proponents of what I taught and continue to teach in my workshops today.

The Power of Sisterhood

The spiritual path was oddly enough found through Facebook. I felt something else calling to me. I made many connections in various Facebook groups. When Mario passed, I went on a quest to find answers. Answers about what happens when we die, but also why our human bodies get sick. I wanted to change our diets. I watched this awesome documentary called *Crazy Sexy Cancer* and I took on the thought that plant-based diets were the cure for it all. I met a woman named Gina online. I spoke to her about helping me in terms of nutritional changes. I couldn't afford her consultation fee at the time, but the two of us became friends. She taught me to connect to my intuitive nature again. She gave me an incredible reading and one by one each of the things she spoke about began happening. One day she called me and asked me if I wanted to be part of a circle of women who got together weekly to meditate and plant dreams. I had never heard anything like it, but it sounded quite amazing to me.

I met so many women in all different parts of the country and the world. Each week I looked forward to our time together. As the months went on, I got to meet so many of them in person. These women gave me wings to fly. They reminded me of my power, and their collective energy fueled my dreams. I felt so utterly supported. I grew to love each and every one of them. Their meditations, music, songs, and dances. They let me into their hearts and some of them their homes. You don't meet people like these ladies every day. They reminded me of the magic of sisterhood, the magic in the world, and the magic in me—for that I will always be eternally grateful. It was another reminder for me that family is not always what you think it is and that having female friendships is so important.

Trust the Reroute

Around this time, monarch butterflies began to appear once again. This time along my commute during another big transitional phase in my life. One that I felt I was being thrust into this time and not of my own choosing. I was a contract speech therapist at a school for children with special needs. The school administration was transitioning to only keeping full-time employees on staff, terminating all per diem therapists like me. As a now single mom, staying at the school would have meant taking a pay cut and not dropping off or picking up my daughters from school. It just was not an option for me.

I remember calling a colleague crying; I was so frightened and uncertain of what the future would bring. Later, a single conversation I had with my supervisor (where I was being fired essentially), altered the entire trajectory of my life. It led to me studying educational administration, which led to my journey into learner-centered education, which eventually led to me unschooling[3] my daughters and traveling across the country with them—just the three of us. A trip that I can confidently say made up the best seven weeks of my life—hands down. Looking back, it was like the butterflies were whispering: "Just let it all go. Everything is going to be okay."

This is just another example of how if you stay somewhere too long, life will force you to leave. Getting fired was the best thing that ever happened to me the first time and now it was happening again.

---

3. Unschooling is the idea that children can direct their own learning, at their own pace, without the rigid structures of formal education.

Fly Forward and Let Go

There's no way Nick would have let me go across the country. We were not on the greatest of terms. But remember my sisters from the meditation circle? They made me believe I could do anything. While some people were telling me I was crazy, they were reminding me that I was brave, inspiring, and bad ass. Who are you going to listen to? That question is so important. I used energy. I used intention. I wrote Nick a letter thanking him for letting me go, for letting the girls experience this unbelievable journey. I constantly reaffirmed the reality I was creating for myself. Although I never physically gave him the letter, I read it every day until it was a reality. It worked. He agreed to allow me to unschool our girls and take them on this trip of a lifetime.

We had one slight delay as my youngest daughter broke her right tibia sliding down a playground slide. I was in my dress and she was on my lap, and my oldest was shouting: "Just one more time, Mom!" So instead of leaving for our trip as planned, we waited until her cast was off. But during that time, we sent healing energy to her leg, and her cast came off earlier than doctors anticipated. She was still a little unstable because she needed physical therapy for strength. I packed a light umbrella stroller to take with me, and before you knew it my girl was running down hotel hallways.

Because I gave up my apartment and our youngest got injured, we ended up moving back home with Nick until she was well enough for us to continue as planned.

Nick's sister said she'd never let me go if she were him, and luckily she wasn't. This was one of the few times he defended me while I was gone. His family told him I was kidnapping the kids and never coming back. Did I want to never come back? Definitely—so much of my life I felt like I didn't belong. Finding a spiritual community, many who lived out west, I thought maybe that was where I belonged also, but I would never do that to him. I gave him my word and I kept it. I flew him out to California when we got there just in time to celebrate our big girl's eleventh birthday in Disneyland! It all felt like a dream.

Someone said they thought I won the lottery. In many ways I felt like I did. I sold all my belongings. Took a hiatus from work. I worked odd jobs from my laptop at night and used the money I saved from not having to pay rent, my security deposit, and child support I was receiving to make it through those seven weeks.

And everything I gave up was nothing compared to what I received in return. I was worried I would be and feel homeless, but in actuality—as my friend Gina reminded me—I was home free. And I can honestly say I had never felt freer in my life.

I mapped out our adventure loosely based on some pretty big natural wonders and sightseeing and I sprinkled that with meeting up with family and friends. I avoided the Rocky Mountains at all costs because I have a crippling fear of heights.

Our first stop was in Niagara Falls—we stayed in this charming AirBnb in Buffalo, New York. I was greeted by the sweetest old woman who came down to help me with my bags. It was nightfall by the time we arrived, and I remember feeling scared and overwhelmed. It was then that I had my first and only "what the fuck am I doing" moment. But she made me feel like family. Like I was a niece or something coming to visit. During our stay, I asked if we could extend our trip by one extra night and she said of course. Her warmth was the little push I needed. She was definitely an angel on my path.

The falls were incredible. We then went on to visit the Great Lakes Science Center in Cleveland, Ohio, situated on Lake Erie. Next we headed to Detroit, Michigan, where we stayed with my older cousin Mario—on Mario's birthday—synchronicity! He took us to the Ford Museum and to the farm so we could carve pumpkins with the girls. We learned to make paper airplanes, how to put together a Model T car and sat on Rosa Parks's bus!

Next stop was to the outskirts of Chicago where Nick had an aunt. She too kept reminding me how brave I was and was thankful for visitors as she didn't get many from New York since she made the move several years prior. We went to Navy Pier, the Shedd aquarium where we met Nickel the sea turtle, and to the DuPage Children's Museum. The girls were getting so many unforgettable hands-on experiences! From there we went horseback riding in Indiana. Next, we made our way to the St. Louis Arch in Missouri. We learned about the westward expansion and Lewis and Clark. I was too scared to go into the actual arch, but my oldest wanted to go and those were the things that made me sad about being a single mama. Having a dad would have made certain aspects easier. But I didn't let it get me down. Interestingly enough, we ran into a homeschool group on our adventure. The girls took a class with other home-schoolers and we visited a home that was built entirely by slave labor. It was so emotional. We also visited the first brick house west of the Mississippi River. There was so much education happening during our travels my girls could never learn in any history book.

We carried on and made our way to Memphis, Tennessee, where the girls and I took the sweetest horse and carriage ride. We traveled south along the Mississippi River. Our next stop was in New Orleans where I splurged for a more expensive hotel in the safer part of town, and we took in the sights and sounds of the French Quarter. The girls didn't really love the night vibe there, but we had the most delicious beignets, took a tour on one of those double decker buses, and had the funniest guide!

We then visited our friend Michael in Dallas, Texas. She was part of my women's meditation group. She opened her home to us despite never meeting me in person before. She gave me one of the most incredible hugs I have ever received from a friend. I remember something shifted inside me when I got to Texas. It felt like the air was different, crisper, cleaner. Believe it or not, this is when it really hit me . . . I drove all the way to Texas! How incredible? Just a little indication of how disconnected I still was within myself among the enormity of situations. Sometimes I think if I really understood the magnitude of what I was taking on, I never would have pulled out of that driveway on October 24, 2013.

The girls and I eventually made our way over to Roswell, New Mexico—the cutest alien town—and witnessed one of the most incredible sunsets I have ever seen on the drive across the border. We were traveling as the sun was going down, and I just felt so surrounded by all this incredible beauty. It was like a huge hug from Mama Nature. "Two Tickets to Paradise" was playing on the radio, and it could not have been more perfect. After New Mexico, we went to visit an old friend in Chandler, Arizona. She took us to Scottsdale, and I knew we just had to see the Grand Canyon! Even though I had been there years before, it was something I knew my girls needed to experience. You can imagine how tired they were of museums, aquariums, and just sightseeing in general. They told me they had had enough, but I begged them to do this one more thing and they said okay! I am always in awe of how much trust my girls had in me. They didn't question much, they always felt safe when we were together. I knew they didn't realize how lucky they were, and I am happy they did not know anything other than that.

My girls were such troopers. They got up with me before the sunrise with no complaints to drive to a local hotel where the tour bus would be leaving from. Due to my great fear of heights, there was no way I would be driving anywhere near the Grand Canyon myself. I will never forget our tour guide's name; it was Montana. There were only adults in the small passenger bus/van that met us there. I heard grumbles from some of the other guests annoyed that they would be traveling with kids. By the time the tour was over, they were laughing and smiling, surprised at what a joy my girls were and how well behaved. I will never forget the looks on the girls' faces the moment they saw the Grand Canyon—they were so awe inspired and this became my favorite memory of the trip. I was so nervous because there are no railings there and I kept reminding them to stay far enough away from the edge. They were thoroughly enjoying themselves and told me it was worth the pre-dawn wake up call. They cheered me on to climb up to places I was afraid to go. They truly are the most amazing travel companions both literally and figuratively.

Eventually we made it to California! I can't tell you what it felt like to see the "Welcome to California" sign. For a few moments I allowed myself to actually be proud. I remember we were playing old school hip-hop on the CD player as we approached the border. I was truly in awe of myself. We were now just a few days shy of my big girl's eleventh birthday. We had been traveling for almost twenty-four days! Nick flew in—he was not happy—but despite that we took the girls to Disneyland to celebrate. It was indescribably magical; the whole park was decorated for Christmas!

We visited Long Beach Pier as a family. I whispered my wishes to the ocean, and Nick left soon after. The girls and I spent that Thanksgiving in an Earthship[4] situated in a place called Boulder Gardens in Yucca California near Joshua Tree. The land was owned by a man named Garth, who purchased the 640 acres to be closer to nature. My friend Gina, another sister who I met through the women's circle, was living there and invited us to visit. It's hard to describe the experience of being completely surrounded by untouched nature. It is just something you have to witness in order to fully comprehend the overwhelming peace that comes from being in a place like that. These were my second favorite sunsets. We were completely off-grid for almost a week! I could not at all have imagined the memories we would be making before we left. I remember while in California, we went to Venice Beach by day and then ice skating in Santa Monica by night. It was like a dream and California started to really feel more like home than any place I had ever been.

After Nick went back home, I told him I didn't want to come back. I felt like I found something there. The ocean, the vibe, the gardens, and the people. He did not like that idea and became understandably upset, but I promised I would come back and I did. I was hoping his visit would entice him to feel the pull I was feeling, but it did not. I think he believed that I wanted him to love what I envisioned for the girls and me but

---

4. According to Wikipedia, an Earthship is a style of architecture designed to behave as a passive solar earth shelters made of both natural and upcycled materials. Earthships are designed to withstand the extreme temperatures of a desert.

without him in the picture. Because we communicated so poorly, these things were not clearly expressed. Nick was hoping I would move back in with him upon our return (we were home in time for Christmas—as promised), but it didn't feel right because the romantic relationship just was not there for me.

The girls and I trekked together for almost two months, and it transformed me and us in the process. We slept in close quarters most nights, and we created a bond I will treasure for all of my life. Not everyone is courageous enough to do what I did; I fully understand that now. I always had a hard time giving myself the recognition I deserve and at times I still do. Later others would try to taint what we had (namely his sister) and say the girls missed out on a year of school, had trouble acclimating back, and so on. But no one will ever understand the priceless memories we created, but the three of us. The experiences we had were indescribable—no one could ever take those seven weeks with my daughters away from me. I will always cherish it.

And as for them not really being able to truly acclimate back, when I embarked on unschooling I never intended they go back to traditional schooling, but I did promise to give them the choice after giving me a chance to show them a different way of life. I am so grateful they did. I don't think traditional education is the best way to learn and I still don't. Children need the space and the freedom to see learning as a natural extension of life. Life is learning. It is inevitable. Is the structure good? Yes, of course, but being forced to learn from such a small narrow lens in my opinion is hardly education.

But they chose to go back, and I honored that choice. My oldest really missed the only type of education she ever knew and of course the familiarity and the friendships. My youngest, on the other hand, really thrived in a more learner-centered environment and would ask many times to be homeschooled again. She was the kid who when she started school, she asked why she had to sit at a desk all day. I really didn't have a good answer for her. Believe it or not, our trip was the reason why my oldest daughter landed a four-year scholarship to an esteemed all-girl private high school of her choice. And by another beautiful synchronicity of life and all of it coming full circle for me, the man responsible for her to be chosen for this incredibly generous gift, the man on the board of directors who shook my hand and acknowledged the bravery that trip represented on my part after interviewing with my daughter, the man whose name was signed at the end of the scholarship letter, was no other than a beautiful man named . . . Mario.

You're Never Really Off Course

Nick thought we would get back together when we returned. When we didn't, I stayed with my brother and his family in the brief transition period. Part of me thought I would make my dream of moving to California a reality, so I really didn't plan for what would happen when I got back. I was in small quarters with my daughters for almost two months. Our journey in my little Honda Fit and staying in hotel and guest rooms alike, made my brother's seven room cape feel so big. I missed them so much even when they were just upstairs. We developed a bond that felt like the most beautiful thing I had ever known.

But Nick's family wasn't having it. They always found a way to make what I was doing wrong. They insinuated that I wasn't caring for my daughters properly. That my brother's house was too crowded. That my children were being abused.

That their clothes were dirty and other nonsense. This was when I realized even more that his family also looked at me as nothing. Instead of coming to me, they talked behind my back as if I was someone on the street to just gossip about. They never honored me as the mother of their nieces or granddaughters. They projected their own inadequacies onto me. If we were family, why would they not come to me with their concerns? But this was always the case. His family talked critically about me and then Nick would come to me with their thoughts, ideas, and misgivings. I genuinely would wonder if he had any of his own novel opinions.

Eventually my brother's wife grew tired of us too. Our homeschool life and their structured routine didn't mesh well together. In a heated argument, we were asked to leave. That was all I needed to find another place to stay. Just another reminder that life will remove you from where you do not belong. My problem was I didn't feel like I belonged anywhere.

Life Finds a Way of Working Itself Out

We then moved in with my friend Liv. My youngest daughter and her daughter were friends who met in preschool. We were also both single moms. She lived in a beautiful home with a separate apartment, which was fully furnished. Remember when I was asked if I was worried about getting rid of everything and I knew that it would just work out?

The only thing I needed was a bedroom, and my uncle gifted me my Nonna's bedroom furniture. What? How incredible! What a beautiful gesture! I couldn't have planned it out better. I had not seen her furniture since she passed away and now it was going to be in my home! My uncle and my brother personally delivered and unpacked it for me. Life always finds a way of working out.

Now that the girls were back in school, I sat and thought about my life as a school-based speech-language pathologist. I had been doing this for over a decade, and I didn't feel fulfilled. I felt the pull to use my personal experiences to reach kids in a bigger way but also to make a greater impact on the world. At first, I thought I wanted to open my own school, which is what led me to study educational administration in the first place. But as that journey opened me up to discover even greater flaws of traditional education, I decided it was more important to focus on the education of my own children, which led me to unschool the girls.

Now that the year was up, I knew that I wanted to do something bigger. Opening the doors to a school was not the answer. I knew if I created an untraditional educational model, then I would attract like-minded families. But my goal was to reach kids who were like the young girl I had been. I wanted to reach other girls who came from families with no support. Girls who appeared as though they had everything going for them on the outside but slowly dying on the inside. I wanted to be a lifeline to the kids that needed the help but didn't show any outward signs of abuse or neglect. The kids whose parents would not otherwise have access to the resources or even a place in their minds to have awareness of concepts that I felt took too long to know. Also, because of what I went through, I knew there were many children who followed this code of silence in order to mask the shame they carried. The shame that comes with revealing the truth of what your life really is, and, in a backwards crazy way, protecting the abusers themselves in the process and keeping the shame away from your family as a whole and essentially yourself. The keepers of family trauma.

I was working with a relationship coach at this time. He didn't just ask me what I wanted to do, he asked what I would pay to do as a job or profession. I wasn't really sure. I knew I would love to help girls who had been through what I had been through but I didn't feel completely ready. He suggested I make videos on the lessons I would want to leave with my own daughters, and at that moment I knew that was it! I didn't make the videos. Instead I began writing. I started writing about all the lessons I had learned that I felt I learned too late. I imagined that if I had this information earlier, I would have made better and healthier decisions for my life and eventually for my children. This is how *Lessons For My Daughters* was born!

At Liv's house, the girls and I had a little ritual—something I learned from being in the women's circle. Something Nonna inadvertently taught me as well. The power we have to speak things into existence. We did something called planting dreams. We each had dream journals; they were blue with sparkles. We would write in them every night by candlelight. I always talked about having a house on the water. My youngest said she wanted a castle on the beach! She then proceeded to draw a picture of the four of us (me, Nick, her, and her big sister) in front of a house with one of those tall mailboxes. I asked her to change it, knowing how powerful her intentions are, but alas, she did not.

Liv and I helped each other with taking the girls to and from school. We ate dinner together. But she grew tired of us, and it felt like jealousy developed too. After nine months of living together, she asked us to leave as well. It felt like no matter where I went, I just couldn't find my place.

Angels on Our Path

After Liv threw me out, I felt so lost and like I didn't belong. Anything I tried just wasn't right. I met up with Nick. I told him I needed a change. I felt like the girls needed it too. With everything I learned about learner-centered education, I wanted a more untraditional setting for them as well. I knew how much they would benefit. I was thinking of moving north of the city, to Westchester even.

I eventually found Nyack, a quaint little town. It was in Rockland County just a little further north of New York City and above Westchester. It was so charming. There were cafes, art galleries, used bookstores, and vintage diners that were featured in movies. Nestled along the Hudson River, I felt like this could be it. And there was an amazing school for the girls—the Blue Rock school. A place where nature was valued. The girls would go outside into the woods twice a day, teachers went by their first names, there were bean bag options for seats—they could kick their shoes off. It was such a beautiful, relaxed atmosphere where learning was actually the priority—true understanding. No tests and no grades until third grade, and portfolio-based projects and exams.

And then there was Ms. Jean. The home the girls and I moved into was split up into four apartments, and Ms. Jean and I lived next door to each other on the top floor. Remember, the girls and I partook in our routine called "planting dreams" where we would write about our dream life, and my girl said she saw us living in a castle on the beach? When we moved in and I was connecting our cable, the cable guy on the phone could see my house (through Google Earth, maybe?). Making sure he had the right house, he said: "It looks like a castle, right?" "Yes!" The rounded part that looked like a tower from the outside was the wall to our living room and Nyack Beach State Park was just eight minutes down the road. We could see the sunset over the Hudson River out our windows! It really felt like a dream. Like what I had been searching for. It felt similar to what pulled me to California. Only in this instance, the girls were still within driving distance to their dad. I thought it was perfect!

And Ms. Jean and I felt so much love for each other instantly. She truly felt like a soulmate. The girls and I moved in with not much furniture, and I was hosting a get-together for New Year's Eve, and we still didn't have a table. Ms. Jean made some calls, and within a few hours a sweet woman was at my door delivering a table for us to borrow.

Ms. Jean was eighty-four at the time. She was born in Morristown, New Jersey. She attended Brown University in Rhode Island. Later in life, she moved to England with her partner Bernie, which is where their daughter still lives. When we shared the castle together, she was still driving. She took classes at the local college and worked at the sweetest toy shop, where we still treasure the many little gifts she brought home for us. She often cat-sat for us, and she really enjoyed our Oreo's company.

Our time together was unfortunately short-lived, and we were both really sad when we wouldn't be neighbors anymore. Although Nick agreed to the move (because, of course, I went to him immediately), he changed his mind, and before I knew it I was being sued to come home. I knew this was a case of his sister meddling and creating fear in his heart that he would lose us somehow. I honestly wish he would have trusted my intuition on the best way to be a mother to our daughters. Some days I believe that had he kept our relationship between us without constant outside interference, we would have had a chance at the family we both desperately wanted.

Ms. Jean helped us pack up the last few things. We said our goodbyes, and I shut off the lights to my place. When I was pulling out of the driveway for the last time, I looked up and noticed my light was on. I wondered if I had forgotten to turn it off, but I quickly noticed that Ms. Jean was standing at my window watching and waiting for us until we drove away before she went back into her apartment. I could not believe the gift I was given by this woman. This was something my Nonna did every time I left her house. I sometimes wonder if she has something to do with me meeting this lovely woman, who felt like a second grandmother to me.

Some things in life feel meant to be, and they remind you of this hidden magic that we don't see. Some people say you shouldn't move your kids around so much, it's not good, they need stability, and so on, but I wouldn't trade those three months with Ms. Jean for the world. I know my girls are better having known her. I know I am.

It reminds me that we must always acknowledge the angels on our path. Ms. Jean made an impact on my life in such a short time. I really thought I had found it all. Castle on the beach, a view of the Hudson River, arts shops, cafes, an incredible school for my girls, and a chance at having a Nonna again. Unfortunately, life had other plans.

Ms. Jean wasn't on my wish list of things, but she truly was a dream come true. She filled a void I didn't realize I had. She really taught me about love at first sight, and although we were neighbors for only three short months, she taught me so much. She embodied a love so pure just like Nonna did. What an incredible treasure she was to me. We kept in touch after we moved again. We came back for lunch dates at Johnny Cakes and walks to the river.

Ms. Jean was so with it too. She cared about me and supported me in all things *Lessons For My Daughters*. I would always mail her copies of the newspaper articles that were written about us after we moved away.

I remember at one point I kept calling her, and Ms. Jean wasn't answering. I luckily reached our old landlord and found out that Ms. Jean ended up in a nursing home. I tracked her down there. The girls and I were blessed to have the chance to visit her a few more times. We fed her and brushed her hair. We read a very special book to her, which was another beautiful link and synchronicity between us. I had read this particular book in junior high school where I first fell in love with the name in the title and one of the reasons I named my younger daughter that. Ms. Jean happened to have the very same book in her book collection that I read more than twenty-five years prior! What are the chances of that? When I told her the story, she immediately gifted it to my daughter with a beautiful inscription that I will always cherish. Ms. Jean left this world six years later in November of 2021. I was heartbroken that I hadn't seen her in a while, but I know she's flying free and I pray that she also knows just how much she did for me, for all of us.

Two Steps Forward, One Step Back

Financed by his sister, Nick took me to court and forced me back "home." Because of this, I ended up having to commute the girls forty-five miles each way to and from their school. On some nights, I slept at my former marital home to make the ordeal less stressful. I think that is honestly what he wanted all along. Maybe if I fought and stood up for myself, I would have won because I truly felt the education was better suited for our girls, but I always felt so weak against his entire family and their bullying ways. They appointed an attorney for my daughter, and I couldn't imagine putting her through it. Because no matter who wins, the girls always lose in the end, feeling stuck between two different people. So I dropped the dream and went back to what felt like a cage-like existence at the time.

This really crushed my big, dreaming, manifesting heart. How could life show me all the beautiful things I wanted and then take them away? I felt angrier than I had in a long time.

But I realized it was my choice to give in and go back— and that our journey in Nyack was one of the most beautiful gifts we had ever been given, even if it was just for a moment.

My mom said it wasn't about the kids, and it felt like this whole court battle was about me. And you know my mom; she never said much of anything, let alone anything so profound, but this resonated with me. Nick told my girls if they moved, he would never visit. When I agreed to come home, he came out to spend an evening with us almost immediately. We resort to control when we are afraid. I did it a lot and I noticed like my family he and his family did too. When I asked why he fought so hard, he said something along the lines of I was his family also. And while I do appreciate the sentiment, it felt like he was intent on keeping me the same, and simultaneously he kept himself and us from growing too.

Eventually, I ended up back on Long Island in a town named Lynbrook, which ironically is the inversion of Brooklyn. I was choosing between two homes at the time. One in Lynbrook and the other in Long Beach, which you will later see the irony in as well.

Pleasure Is Healing

I met another angel and healer in a man named Daniel, or as I referred to him, Danny, who really helped me to embrace my sexuality. He also taught me how allowing yourself to be seen is transformative.

It's not surprising that a sexual encounter took me away from my body and a sexual encounter helped me to return. In one instance I was unsafe, and in the other I felt gloriously seen and appreciated. This was by far one of the most pleasurable healing experiences.

I remember the first time I saw him. In a professional field dominated by women, I didn't normally meet many men, let alone a strikingly handsome one. As soon as I noticed his beautiful face, I glanced down at his hands and there it was, clear as day—a wedding ring. Danny was off limits.

And with that we continued to become friends, just friends. And the beauty of a strictly platonic relationship is that there's no fakeness. There's no trying to impress. There was simply being yourself, and in being authentic, layers were shed. There was no hiding but rather being witnessed, acknowledged, and validated. These are some of the most powerful transformational tools available to us. Daniel was all those things for me, and I like to think I was for him as well.

We worked in small neighborhood preschools together in the Baisley Park Housing Projects. There wasn't much therapy space. Most of the providers used the same rooms, so we began running into each other a lot. Danny was a special education itinerant teacher or SEIT and I was providing speech language pathology. We shared many of the same students and eventually we began purposely scheduling our sessions to overlap in order to hang out together.

Behind the scenes I was working with yet another life coach, as I often did—trying desperately to become the best version of myself. My coach gave me an assignment: I had to interview the people I spent the most time with and ask them a series of questions in an effort to know and understand myself better. I asked Danny if I could interview him. He was surprised since he didn't see himself as such an important part of my life; however, without us really realizing, we in fact had become close, and we were seeing and speaking to each other almost every day.

One of the questions was about what type of friend I was. To my surprise, Daniel's face got totally flushed when I asked him the question. In that single moment, I stood on the precipice of hearing a few otherwise meaningless words strung together to form a sentence that would dramatically change my life. He shared all the reasons that I was a great friend and then he spoke the syllables that would alter our friendship forever. He said: "I think you're a great friend and, if I wasn't married, I think we would be even *better* friends."

I was floored. I knew at that moment that Danny was just as attracted to me as I had been to him! Neither one of us acted on it as he had made his vows to someone else many years prior to us meeting. But it was wild to think that someone as beautiful as him even looked at me that way. But those words crossed a very fine line and soon my world would be changed forever.

The events that followed are somewhat a blur. How could it be that we went from strictly being friends to doing the unimaginable . . . beginning an affair?

I remember one afternoon we agreed to meet at a Starbucks, not far from where I lived at the time. We arranged that he would follow me one day, after work. He again expressed his attraction and the pull he had to me and something along the lines of "*I don't want to live my whole life never getting to experience this with you.*" I know what you're thinking, this sounds pathetic, but I wanted him just as much as he wanted me. And he was very honest from the get go, he had no intentions of leaving his wife.

So, an affair began and that went on for the next two months until the school year ended. We'd meet up in my apartment and have the most transformational time together. I remember the first time we got together I just couldn't even bring myself to do *it*. We got so far as being completely naked in broad daylight in my bed with no covers. He helped me undress and he just looked at me completely bare and said: "I just want to take this all in, you are so beautiful." No one had ever looked at me like that. No one had ever been so completely and utterly present with me. We lay in bed together for hours, naked, just holding each other.

I guess in my brain I had compartmentalized this thing we were doing during school hours with something that was okay since it remained within the container of work—but, of course, there was the fact that his love and presence felt so healing for me that I didn't want it to end. On one hand, it felt so wrong and yucky because after a certain time of the day we could not communicate. I knew it was never going to go anywhere, but at the same time our meeting and our time together felt so unbelievably right and necessary.

However, the moment that school ended, and he had to make up an excuse to leave his home and lie to his wife to be with me, it was over for me. And believe it or not, it was one of the most painful break-ups of my life. And I guess that's what happens when you have one of those once-in-a-lifetime connections. The entire experience really made me question the whole idea of monogamy at the time. I know it's easy to judge. Believe me, I would have too. Had I not been in the situation myself, I would have never understood. This was the second time I felt like magic had led me to the most exquisite thing that I was just not meant to have—at least not for the long term. The first was when I was led to the most magical Ms. Jean.

Was it really just a test of temptation? If it was, we both failed miserably; however, it felt like so much more. And maybe it's because I've never been with someone so present. The cheesy "nothing else exists when we're together concept" was so viscerally true with Danny. Nothing mattered. I was 100 percent "in the now" when we were together. I got completely lost in his big blue eyes, his strong arms, and in watching him work; there was something about the fact that he worked with children. Children in underserved communities. Children who didn't look like him or me but, like myself, he was so drawn to be a part of educating them. And it was more than that, and we both knew it. We provided so much more than special education services to many of those kids. We were a smile, we were love, we were a constant, we were a safe place for students who may or may not have had that at home. And don't get me wrong. As an educator you can play that role no matter where you work, but because of who I am and where I come from, the idea of school being a safe haven for some (as it was for me) was something that touched my heart. And here I was being a part of that alongside one of the most beautiful men I had ever known to date.

Oftentimes children are thrown into life with adults who don't always have their best interest or who unconsciously are passing down their own wounds. They are not safe, but they have a piece of paper and/or a degree, and they get access to these innocent beings. That's not something I have ever or will ever take for granted. To be in the presence of children is to quite literally to have a direct connection to God and spirit in my opinion. They're far less removed from magic and uncluttered with experience than adults, and I saw my time with them as sacred. There is absolutely so much to learn from these little humans.

I had never before had the experience of being with a man who I was attracted to on so many levels. He helped the children. Oh my God, it was the biggest turn on. I experienced things with him in ways that I never have before. With that level of connection comes an excavation of sorts. We can't allow the deepest parts of ourselves to be seen and touched without consequences, can we? And while I know it was an unhealed version of both of us that would even allow us to cross such a sacred boundary—one that I would never come close to doing today—it truly healed me on so many levels but not without consequence.

The Next Step Will Always Reveal Itself

One day, shortly after the affair had ended (it was the next school year), I was driving from one school to the next (because I often visited multiple schools in a day). I made a phone call to my oldest daughter from the car. I can't remember why she was home (it was a school day), and she wasn't answering the phone. I called her dad. He also couldn't reach her. I decided to immediately reroute my drive home to check on her. I started imagining the unimaginable. I started thinking: "What if someone broke into my apartment?" "What if someone is hurting her?" And then, almost automatically, the most profane thought entered my mind: "What if someone is raping her?" Oh my God! How could I even put the most violating fear onto the image of the most perfect essence, my most beautiful, precious daughter?

But the truth is because this was my experience, this was always my fear for them. At the exact moment that this most disgusting thought entered my mind, the people in the image became transposed immediately—and then it was me being raped by my father with my mother watching. All of this took place in a matter of seconds in my brain, but it somehow felt like eternity at the same time.

I was coming to a red light. At that moment, my body went numb. I couldn't hear the world around me; it was the most eerie silence but with a ringing in my ears. I felt like I was going to throw up. In what felt like the same exact instant, my mind shut it off—the image was gone. It was instantaneous. I was disoriented. I had no idea what had just happened. Was it some crazy intuitive vision, or was it a very, very clear flashback? I knew the answer, but I also didn't want to know. Time seemed to stand still. I don't know how I didn't get into an accident. I don't remember stopping. I thought, "This was what it must have been like as a child for me, my mind shutting off and saving me from the reality of the nightmare that was my life."

This flashback inevitably led me to yet another level of healing. The heart-penetrating sex from the previous year felt like it opened some sort of portal. It felt like memories were leaking out of me and there was nothing I could do to contain them any longer. Fear set in. I panicked. All I knew was I didn't want to know. I didn't think I could handle it. I started feeling paranoid. I started questioning everything. Did this really happen? How could this happen? Did anyone know? Did my brother know the extent of this? Did my aunt and uncle who lived next door know? Did my cousins know? Did the neighbors know? Oh my God, did Nonna know?

I had no idea what was going on. I didn't know what was real or what was imagined. I needed help. I started calling everyone I knew. A friend of mine gave me the number to his therapist. She was a sweet woman based out of Washington, DC. She told me I should try EMDR (Eye Movement Desensitization and Reprocessing) and helped me find a practitioner. She directed me to another woman, Susan. When I spoke with Susan on the phone, she shared that she had been through sexual abuse as well. I thought I had found the person to help me. I thought, "Yes, she can relate." I was very wrong.

Not All Therapists Are Created Equal

Although my friend's therapist recommended EMDR (a form of psychotherapy that was designed to alleviate the distress associated with traumatic memories), I ended up with a practitioner practicing RET (Rapid Eye Technology). While in some ways different, both utilize rapid eye movements in connection with going back in time and bringing up old memories while focusing on external stimuli. In my case, it was a wand with an eye at the end of it. It sounds super creepy in a way, but I was desperate for help. For this reason, I did not do any additional research—a big mistake.

Reliving old experiences, especially those you may have completely blocked out, seemed like a terrible idea, but Susan assured me that I would not be re-traumatized. I am not sure if it was the practice itself or the practitioner or both, but my therapist felt predatory in her own right. She kept me in her office for sometimes three hours at a time. She went on and on about how long it would take me to heal because she had never worked with someone with the deep level of trauma I had been through. She basically kept reiterating the fact that I was so damaged and broken. She established herself as the key to "hopefully" overcoming the despair I was in.

I kept trying to piece together the timeline of my life, and she made me feel like every event was due to trauma. She made me question myself as a sexual person even more. Questioning whether I could ever really enjoy sex when it was connected to all this pain. She made me question my natural childhood sexual curiosity and made me feel as if all of it was a result of whatever disturbing things were going on at home. Certainly, it was natural to be curious about your body, sex, and pleasure as a child, right? I had to google it to be sure but regardless of anything I read, my mind felt more in a jumble than ever before. I couldn't decipher normal from abnormal, and she seemed to only make matters worse.

In hindsight, I truly believe she created more harm than good. She made me question every single person in my family. She stirred up really disturbing visions for me. She tried to take me to a time in my life before the trauma and I couldn't access it. I became more and more afraid. I had visions of myself as a young child outside my house in a blood-tattered dress. Things that I had no conscious memories of. It was completely distressing. I became a shell of myself. I came home from therapy and crawled into the fetal position for hours and was in a dissociated state for days. My daughters were frightened.

I cut off my birth family completely during this time. With so much that I was reliving, I had to distance myself from everyone in order to heal. Susan also had me feeling confused, and I felt unsure of anyone I could trust. I questioned who knew and who didn't know of the abuse, although she seemed absolutely sure and kept repeating to me that all these people in my life were bad. I felt isolated, alone, and dark.

Unfortunately, cutting off my brother kept me from my nephews, my favorite boys, something I didn't think of as a possibility. Although it made sense from his perspective, it devastated me completely. When I was doing that project with my life coach and Danny, I interviewed some family members too. My brother had shared with me what a light I represented for those boys. I hate the idea that they think I abandoned them in any way. Aside from my daughters, they were the other most important people in my life.

I never spoke to my father again. My brother and mother were enraged that I stopped speaking to them. The name calling and mudslinging ensued. It was so disappointing. I felt betrayed by my family because again what they needed was more important than my well-being.

At one point, Susan got upset with me over a late payment I made to her. I was paying out of pocket for sessions, and I was having a hard time keeping up financially. She accused me of never mailing a check and trying to take advantage of her. It was like a switch flipped inside her, and she became so nasty towards me. I am so grateful, however, because it allowed me to see her true colors and I never spoke to her again. And while it was in my best interest to stay away from her, I was again left alone and unsure how to deal with all this pain. And it wasn't just what I thought I knew about my life; it was now compounded with all this new information I was given.

More Angels on the Path

One afternoon, after I severed ties with Susan, I ran into one of my oldest daughter's friend's moms. Her name was Lucia. Our girls went to private school together for elementary school and junior high. I enrolled my daughters in private school when I realized that I didn't really love the public school system in our community. And although it was a beautiful school and a great education, I never really felt like I fit in. The large majority of families were members of the local country club, and that just wasn't a place I personally felt comfortable. I was also one of the few moms whose child was their oldest child. Most of the girls in my daughter's grade were for some reason the youngest sibling so I was a lot younger than most of the moms. This one mom in particular, Lucia, was sort of the mother hen. She was older, wiser, so put together, well spoken, and well off. I didn't really think she liked me nor did I ever think we could have much of anything in common.

Our paths crossed again when both of our daughters ended up in an all-girl private high school together. We were both at a holiday fair where I was showcasing my work with *Lessons For My Daughters*. So, when we ran into each other on this particular day, we somehow got on to that subject. I am not entirely sure why Lucia decided to open up to me that day, but she went on to share the nightmare that was her own life. I could never ever have dreamed, not even for a second, that woman who seemed to have it all—great husband, family, career, wealth—had any experience with some of the awful things I had gone through yet she did. It's so true what they say: never judge a book by its cover—truly everyone has a story. I envied Lucia because she seemed to have found success in the area of relationships and family despite the chaos that was her life in a way I never could.

She took me to dinner one night soon after. I told her about my experience with RET and Susan. Lucia reminded me that my experience with Susan was not normal and not okay! It is amazing how years later we still cannot see dysfunction for what it is because of the way we grow up. Lucia seemed to take me under her wing. She felt like a big sister. She had actually heard of other people's negative experiences with Susan. She made a call immediately and connected me to her therapist Janet, who wasn't taking any more clients but did so as a favor. Two more angels on my path.

I will never know why Lucia took an interest in helping me. She was only in my life for a short time. After I slipped into the darkest phase of my healing, we sort of drifted apart and she passed away sadly a few years after that. I know I have thanked her many times, but I hope she knows just how much her presence in my life, regardless of how short, meant to me.

While there is not a lot of literature on RET specifically, it is a form of EMDR. And while most research shows EMDR to be safe and effective, it is important to do your own research and determine what is best for you. You will be hard pressed to find much negative information; however, I have since spoken to many women on the topic as well as other professionals. Some women felt the modality changed their life in positive ways, and others who felt the therapy was a step backward for them like it was for me (although I still believe Susan played a big role in that). I have also spoken to other practitioners who shared that it isn't always the best course for people with complex trauma.

Here are some things that can happen as a result, none of which were discussed with me: the surfacing of additional traumatic memories, and strong, intense emotions during and after the sessions, lasting from hours to days. An overall sense of feeling more emotionally sensitive and vulnerable, discomfort during sessions, such as experiencing physical sensations (i.e., muscle tension), tearfulness, or anger, vivid dreams, and feeling extremely tired after sessions. It is important to discuss what comes up for you and if any of it does or doesn't feel right to you. Speak with your therapist, and if they don't listen to your concerns, please move on. When trauma is all we know, unfortunately we tend to get ourselves into these situations, especially when we are desperate to heal.

The Wound Is Where the Light Enters

I would never in a million years dream that Nick became dependent on prescription pain medication. Eventually he told me that people liked him better when he was on them. He also said that they made him feel like who he was meant to be. That made me so sad at the time, and while I assured him that wasn't true, it was something he really believed. No one wanted to interact with him while on a mind-altering substance, yet I could understand why he felt that way. In our marriage I never knew why he always seemed unhappy and depressed. I didn't understand what his mood swings and anger were really about. How could I when I didn't fully understand my own trauma at the time? But we truly did trigger each other's pain. In many ways, this is the inevitability of intimate relationships: they bring us our greatest insecurities but if you don't know what to do with that, it really is a recipe for disaster.

Nick and I became the things we didn't want to be. Finding out about Nick's addiction devastated and crushed me. Believe it or not, his family told me about it. He ultimately became unrecognizable to me, which was one of the scariest things I had to go through. Despite all of our ups and downs, he was the only family I had ever known and during that time I felt like I was losing that too. Sure, we had not been together in a long time, but emotionally we were always entangled—many would even call it trauma bonded.[5]

In the end he told me that I was so cold in our marriage and, although I couldn't see it, he was right. He told me I resembled his mom to him, and I know that I subconsciously punished him for my experiences with my father.

The night that changed my life forever was when he told me that he "fucking hated me" and wished we had never met. Even though, believe it or not, we had said similar things to each other in the past, this was different. The fury in his voice pierced me right down to my very core. We were already ten years post-divorce by then, just to give you some perspective on how energy trumps manmade paper and agreements and the dissolvement of said agreements. It didn't matter, I was still very much connected to him but not in a healthy way.

The day after this exchange, Nick told me he loved me. Those two conflicting statements sent my nervous system

---

5. Trauma bonding is a type of attachment that one can feel toward someone who's causing them trauma—physical, emotional, sexual. It brings with it not only feelings of sympathy, compassion, and love, but also confusion.

into a tailspin. I think he triggered something really deep and ugly from my past. The incongruence between loving someone and then causing them the most deep, penetrating, and long-lasting pain was something my mind could not handle. Not again.

It took me doing things wrong so many times to finally start understanding the patterns. For me, it was great pain that led me to the hardest lessons, which then led to the most incredible transformations.

Codependency and Trauma

I began learning about codependency. Believe it or not it was Nick's mother and sister who helped me tremendously over this time. You would think this was a positive thing and in many ways it was however much of it was a pattern too. It seemed that they were only capable of being there for me when I was on my knees in pain. Almost like they got something out of helping me at my lowest, yet were never around to bask in my success or celebrate me in good times. My former mother-in-law happened to be the only person in the world I knew who could understand what I was going through because she also married a man who struggled with addiction. She introduced me to Nar Anon, and that was my first step at beginning to really set boundaries. It was a godsend learning about codependency and all the things that go along with it. I met other people who were going through similar things and that is always so helpful. I learned about detachment even though it would be a little while before I could actually implement it. And while having my ex-mother-in-law and ex-sister-in-law to talk to helped me so much, at the same time it felt really self serving. They were benefitting from the private information and details of what was happening with Nick that I shared with them in which I foolishly thought was in confidence. There were never clear-cut boundaries, and when I confided in them on various things, my confidence was always betrayed because to them I was always an outsider and this situation was just another reminder of that.

Lesson Still Not Learned

Around this time, so much was going on. My life was a mess because a man who was once my best friend was becoming unrecognizable to me. Deaths and rebirths were occuring on multiple levels. I was also being evicted from my apartment as a result of poor decisions I made with Nick as my consultant. Was this a way for him to once again get us back home? It sure seemed that way. After searching endlessly for a suitable home for our daughters without any luck, eventually I *again* moved back into our marital home at his suggestion. This was another huge mistake. I mean, even writing it down seems absolutely ridiculous. How did it seem that I was going back-wards another time? My oldest daughter said it was a bad idea and she was usually right about these things, but I was truly and utterly exhausted. I was tired of being a single mother. I was tired of shouldering all the financial responsibilities. I told myself it was temporary, but part of me also believed that it could work out this time. I mean, that's all I ever wanted—a happy family under one roof. Despite the fact that this put a strain on my relationship with my oldest, I felt like I needed a break and there we were back in the blue house on the corner once again.

Life Will Continue to Push
You Toward Healing

Things were going okay. I mean I can't remember a time where Nick and I *ever* really displayed a true appearance of being happy and in love. I really don't remember many times like that when we were actually married either. The moments were very few and far between. But things were going okay and I learned not to expect much else. We had spent months planning one of the most beautiful celebrations for our oldest daughter's Sweet Sixteen. It was November 2018. Every little detail was accounted for, and thousands of dollars were spent.

I eventually began making amends with my family . . . slowly. I gave my daughter the option of having her nonna there, and she did. We invited her. You would think she would have been a resounding yes right way, but she said she had to think about it. She did eventually agree to attend. We also invited my nephews; however, I wasn't ready to make peace with my brother. The strain on that relationship has always been different. I saw my brother as my ally, my contemporary. We were in this together, weren't we? Out of everyone in the world, he was the only other person who could possibly get it. But he didn't or maybe he just couldn't. He didn't come, and I couldn't invite him.

I felt too betrayed. When he's angry and hurt, my brother always lashes out, and he says some really terrible things. Of course, I know I hurt him too because I questioned the safety of my children around his presence. But my therapist—Susan— told me that when people protect predators, they are predatory themselves, and it seemed right and truly felt that way. I did what I thought was best at the time. My only regret is that I hurt my nephews. My brother was never the person to sit with me and try to figure out my pain or be with me in it or help me to make sense of my life, so I did not really feel bad for him. He had the "get over it and move on" mentality when it came to me only and that's just not how trauma works.

The boys were given the option to come, and all three of them *wanted* to be there. That made my heart so happy. All I ever really wanted was to have my nephews in my life, and I was grateful they were not going to miss out on their cousin's Sweet Sixteen.

The night before the party, Nick took us shopping for jewelry. He was remarkably happy. He was sweating. I didn't want to see it but I knew. I asked him about it when he got home. He told me he slipped up but he had it under control. I began to cry. He swore he would not take anything at the party and I believed him. I am not sure it was true but, regardless, it truly was one of the most special nights of my life.

Although his family was still "his family"—they interrupted my speech and his sister of course would not give me the recognition of a job well done—for a few hours, it felt like the four of us were really solid.

Emerging Butterfly

Moving On for Good

It didn't stay that way and I can use the word unfortunately here but it has taken me a long time to realize and actually be at peace with the fact that it was not meant to be. Nick and I tried couples therapy with this really awesome woman. She was a licensed marriage and family counselor. I didn't realize that many therapists practiced as such but didn't actually take the extra required coursework to get certified. Even though this wasn't the first time we had tried couples counseling, I felt like this was the first time we were both *really* invested. Nick committed to recovery but I always had my doubts. Seeing him in that way was a traumatizing experience that always left me on high alert. Aside from that, the therapist also told me he would not emotionally connect to me the way I needed him to, and I knew she was right: not because he wasn't capable but just because of all the damage we had done to each other over the years. On top of that, a few members of his family and I had a falling out over another familiar situation. Them talking about me and my daughters behind my back and Nick going along with it reminding me where his true loyalty would always be. His top concern was always his family of birth and not the one he created and it would make sense because they were so enmeshed but I had to break free of this pattern once and for all. On New Year's Eve of 2018, I told him that I would not go into another year cycling through the same old patterns, and I ended it with him for good. I cried and cried. He was so upset too, but I genuinely did not have the answers nor the tools to make it work. I cried so many tears that created a headache that lasted into the new year.

Complete Deconstruction

Anxiety doesn't come from nowhere. I don't care how young or old you are. Your body remembers and carries everything, all the pain and trauma from the past. Always communicating with you and has been all along. Perhaps you weren't listening or maybe you just weren't ready. It's here now. It's at the forefront. Don't stuff it down. Be brave enough to face it. And even though the idea that our body remembers everything can be frightening, you are capable. You *can do it*.

For me, my body showed up screaming at me. She also showed up in another person.

I fucking hate you. I wish I had never met you!

Remember? That's what the father of my children said to me in what seemed like a drug-induced rage. Little did I know that those few words would knock my nervous system completely off center and not return to homeostasis for another eleven months.

I was trying to talk him out of taking our youngest daughter in his car while he was intoxicated. He was taking her to his friend's house whom he was house sitting for. He and my youngest, all alone, while he was God knows where in his mind. I couldn't allow it. I had to stand up to him. I had to protect our daughter. I had to protect her as no one ever did for me! He was totally fine and totally capable—that's what he said.

I was no match for him. When he was irate, I became a little girl and froze. Despite my best efforts to stop him, Nick took off with her that night, and I ended up taking our oldest out for dinner in lieu of the mother-daughter night she did not want to attend that evening. I remember it was rainy, and there was a chill in the air.

I kept in touch with my baby girl all through the night via text. When I dropped my oldest off at home, I went back to physically check on them. He invited me over to his friend's house, where he was staying, and I heard him talking to someone on the phone. He always made lots of phone calls and was very animated when he was high.

Our daughter was fine and didn't seem to notice anything out of the ordinary. I don't know if that's good or bad. Nick had bought her a ton of candy and sugary treats, and she seemed content. And . . . it turned out that he had to go to the hospital. He had recently noticed an infection on his leg and it had gotten worse.

He was admitted that night and I took our daughter home. The next day I took her back to visit Nick. He was hooked up to an IV drip and pain medication. He was now a completely different person. So calm, so nice. He was having a pleasant conversation with one of his brothers over the phone. I didn't understand why only I seemed to get the worst part of him—at least that was how I interpreted it. Also why did I make myself continuously available for that? As we were leaving, he said he loved me and that is what really did it. The contrast between the "I fucking hate you" the night before and the current "I love you"—my brain just could not make sense of the two phrases. Especially not from a man whom I actually thought would *always* love me. Two complete opposite sentiments in the span of two days. It just couldn't be, I thought. It could not be that you indeed love me! You just told me you hated me. You just said you wish you had never met me. The two phrases brought me straight back to my mind as a child. It was the only thing that can logically explain what happened next . . . what felt almost like a psychotic break.

How could the people who love you the most cause you the most psychological, physical, and emotional damage? How could it be? How could pleasure and pain almost be one in the same? This also brought up for me one of my most enormous wounds: believing anyone actually truly loves me and has my back one hundred percent and again he was proving my erroneous belief that it was just not possible for me to have that.

And so it began, the sound of Nick's voice would now send me into a literal panic attack. I was so frightened. How could the one person I had always relied on be the one who was making me sick? Had he always been making me sick and now my body and psyche had had too much? Had I been in this toxic dynamic for too long and my body was saying NO MORE? Or was he merely just the physical representation for the pain that I carried all along?

You cannot heal in the same environment that made you sick.
You cannot heal in the same environment that made you sick! That
was all that I kept hearing in my mind.

I don't really believe he was *making* me sick, in fact the
situation that was presenting itself was truly the catalyst to the
next stage in my healing. No one can or should have that kind
of power over you, especially as a grown adult, however we
have to see the role we are playing in it. That awareness is the
key. Owning your choices empowers you to see that you are the
one in control to put an end to it. Ultimately you are responsible for the cycles you are choosing to participate in.

Walking away from my relationship with Nick that felt
like it was slowly KILLING me was the most painful lesson I
had to learn. But every time you walk away from what doesn't
serve you—you become equally more open to RECEIVING
and also more POWERFUL.

My Body Screaming to Me

On April 14, 2019, I had a panic attack that lasted over
twenty-four hours. It was triggered by Nick's words. Twenty-
one years of relating with him and his family in a way I was
familiar with—dysfunctional. And although it may have
been glaringly obvious to everyone else, I didn't have a real
clue to the extent of it all. I am certain my friends were tired
of hearing my repetitive stories over and over again. Although
logically I knew something was off, it felt absolutely impossible to break away from this dynamic after being inside it for
so long.

Nick was someone who, I thought, if he could just change,
everything would be better. I would be better, we would be

happy, and our family would be perfect (by "our" I meant the one we created together). I was so enmeshed in this unhealthy relationship that I no longer knew who I was without it. I didn't know where he ended or where I began. He was a part of my identity, and the way I related him to me was like a heavy garment cemented into my soul.

I remember trying to sit at my computer typing speech evaluation reports the night before the panic began; the screen itself was making me feel nauseated. I decided I would just go to sleep early in the hopes that I would feel better when I woke up. I got up extra early to finish what I could not complete the night before; this was not out of the ordinary because procrastination was my middle name at the time. It didn't work. I felt so off, unable to get myself to return to a feeling of "normal." I called 9-1-1 in the early hours of the next morning because it truly felt like I was dying. I asked the operator to stay on the phone with me until help arrived. She couldn't give me her name, but she was such an angel.

The police and EMS tried to convince me to go to the hospital, but I just needed to know my vitals were okay. I could not let my girls wake up to me not being there—especially when their father was coincidentally in the hospital.

As soon as it seemed like not such an ungodly hour, I phoned my friend Heather, and she stayed on with me until I felt the slightest bit better. Thank goodness she answered the phone, another angel. As the sun came up, and it got a little more into the day, I called my therapist to make an appointment, but she couldn't see me until the late afternoon. Not functioning well with too much idle time, I showed up to her place an hour early and just sat barefoot on the grass outside her office—not caring about what passersby might think. I did whatever I could possibly do to feel better, but everything I had in my toolbox just was not working for me.

I had never experienced this feeling of being so uncomfortable in my own body (that I could consciously remember). This was the first clue to how disconnected with myself and my body I truly was and how disconnected I had been from the trauma that took place all those years before. I did yoga. I googled meditations upon meditations upon meditations. I listened to affirmations. I had that therapy session. It was somewhat helpful but inside I felt like I was spinning out of control. My mind was racing.

After twenty-four painfully long hours of feeling every single minute fully, I thought I needed medication. I went to a doctor whom I had never met, and she wrote me two prescriptions (one was for Xanax and the other for an anti-anxiety medication), but I was so afraid to take them. I took just one of the anti-anxiety meds and it made me feel sick. I called my therapist, and she said that it was impossible to feel the effects of them so soon and that I should calm down and give them a chance to work over time. I couldn't do it. They remained in my drawer—almost like a safety net—until I was able to throw them away almost a whole year later. There's nothing wrong with needing medication, but due to my upbringing I had a lot of negative views around it. There was a part of me that wanted to know that I could conquer whatever was happening to me without numbing any part of myself in any way.

The next few months were exhaustive and frightening. I felt like I was in a dark hole that I would never get out of. Every moment I thought I was dying. In fact, I knew if I told any medical professional what I was really feeling, they would certainly recommend the psychiatric ward.

What I didn't realize is that I was on a path of breaking down all the erroneous beliefs I had about myself, relationships, relating—about everything! So much would fall away that at one point I would no longer recognize myself. But at that time, it was so hard to see beyond the pain and fog I was living in daily.

During this time, I was teaching my *Lessons For My Daughters* workshop at the junior high school I attended as a tween, which was the age I felt I was in the height of the abuse (but since there are so many gaps in my memory I can never be sure). I just remember driving into the neighborhood I grew up in with such fear of having some sort of flashback. The timing of it all seemed so strange. I had to cancel one class, which was something I had never done before and haven't had to since, but the amazing thing I did realize was that teaching always brought me back to homeostasis. Teaching was healing to me because I was able to share the truth of myself as a gift to others, and it made me feel balanced once again. Years later a woman I would meet, Erika, shared that this meant I was living my dharma (my purpose in life). I miraculously finished out that series. Everyone involved in the coming to fruition of that workshop felt like more angels on my path.

Be Willing to Face Yourself

Through this journey of healing, I revisited every bad thing I believed about myself. That I indeed was crazy. That I would end up in a mental hospital like my father did. That I would spend my life reliant on medication. That none of it was real or a big deal (just like my parents made me believe and doubt myself). I had nightmares. I couldn't sleep. I constantly felt like my heart was beating outside of my chest, pounding uncontrollably. That sensation woke me up nightly in a panic and sweat for what seemed like no apparent reason. But nothing happens for no reason. Your body is always speaking to you and a lot comes up in the silence, the void.

I quickly realized that my body would relive all her inner little girl trauma in the stillness of the dark. Whenever I tried to rest, she woke me up, asking me to remember. She was ready to feel it, but I really wanted no part of it. I was never more scared in my life. Or maybe I was and this was showing me the way I really felt back then.

There's a reason why we are constantly moving and longing to be distracted, and why there are so many external things designed to distract us, to keep us numb, to not to feel, and to not to be silent and alone with our thoughts, our past, our memories. Things we have not processed, things we are afraid to face and secretly keep tucked away. It's because we are truly afraid to face ourselves. To look at ourselves through a clear lens is quite possibly the most frightening of all journeys. But remember the magic that happens in the dark, and if you choose to ignore it, you're missing out on living life in a deep and powerful way.

They're not lying when they say, the only way out is through. Sometimes for so long you forget the pain is even there. That's what happened to me. I forgot it was there. I didn't even consciously remember the profoundness of it, but my body would not allow me to forget and she was ready to face it. The only choice I had was to surrender.

In every moment, it felt as if death was upon me. One minute, I'd be fine and the next minute I'd feel as if every nutrient I needed to survive was rapidly draining from my body. I had to face the deepest, darkest unhealed parts of myself. I had to tell that little girl inside me that I believed her and that I would not silence her any longer. She was so angry and rightfully so. I had to truly understand without a doubt that I was the only answer to my coming back to wholeness. We look so desperately outside of ourselves for the key, but you are the only thing that can truly bring you there.

And the thing is, that little girl, she really just wanted to be acknowledged in a way she never was. Just like the monarch, we come equipped with an inner compass. It is so much sharper when we are young before the world tells us who and what we should be. Little me needed big, grown-up me to finally acknowledge that my dismissing that inner knowing hurt me then, and it was still hurting me now.

And through and through, I will tell you the most powerful thing that helped me to heal and get back to myself. Not my old self—a new integrated, validated self. It was those people who kept reminding me that I was indeed *NOT* crazy. That I would get through this. That it was normal to be feeling this way. Anyone who had gone through such a violent life would feel this way! More angels. My friend Teresa reminded me that eventually I would look back at this like a short blip in time. As hard as it was to believe then, the more time that passed, the truer it became.

And I'm here to remind you, that you too are not crazy. You are not what happened. I believe you and there is a light at the end of what sometimes feels like this long ass, never-ending tunnel. And guess what? You are that light!

For a long time, the simple telling of *this* story scared me. Facing the trauma seemed more traumatic than the trauma that I kept hidden! Not intentionally, not consciously, but as a safety measure. You see, being disassociated was what helped me survive; it was what kept my spirit intact, then. At the time it was necessary and a gift. It kept safe the part of the caterpillar that makes its way into those beautiful wings. It can never be taken away—the real me. But now it was time to integrate the two and really soar.

The Answers Are Within You

It is most important to find a modality you connect with, personally. Like I said, there are many routes to the same destination. See what works for you. What nudges are on your path right now? Have several different people mentioned the same thing to you? Learn to recognize and listen to the signs. Learn to trust your intuition. When the student is ready, the teacher appears; the next step will always be there waiting. Also trust that when someone or something is not good for you, you will know it. If it is making you feel worse, like Susan did for me, it is most likely not for you.

Some people's work doesn't seem to fit under any of these umbrellas. For example, Iris's work moved me in a way that is hard to explain. She called herself a spiritual teacher and I can tell you with certainty, I don't know what I would have done without this woman. I signed up for a reading with her, and the only date available fell around the time I was in such a dark place, even though I was "fine" when I made the appointment.

I ended up working with her one on one. I can tell you with certainty that the biggest part of her magic was that Iris never did the work for me. She just intuitively knew what questions to ask and she pointed me to my own healing. She taught me that I could do it all myself. She reminded me of my power, my divinity, my connection to everything. She just kept telling me that what I was experiencing was normal based on what I had been through. My body was remembering, releasing. My whole life was coming to a head. She never told me I was crazy. She never said this was too big a mountain to climb (which is what the RET therapist repeatedly told me).

I remember one day we had a phone session scheduled, and I didn't even have enough breath in my body to speak. Iris asked me what I needed, and I told her I just needed her to talk to me. She sat on the phone and poured love into me. I wish everyone could understand how much our words and presence have the power to heal as well as our energy and intention. She had BIG Nonna love and really a gift.

I learned more than ever the importance of what to put into my body as a source of nourishment. To listen to my body. At this point in time my body was being so strict and what felt unforgiving at the time. I couldn't eat anything bad for me or I would feel it in the worst way. I learned the true meaning of "let food be thy medicine, and let medicine be thy food."

Iris also helped me to get my thoughts out onto paper, an action that used to be so scary for me to do. Although I have always been a writer, there's something so permanent about putting words on paper that it has always been frightening to me. It was like almost admitting the reality of my experiences. If I write it down, then it must be true. But really, writing is just another way of moving the energy through you into something else. That is the most important thing to learn; our memories, experiences, thoughts, they're like living things and they need a way to be expressed. Can you imagine what it would be like if they never found a way out? I lived that nightmare.

Iris encouraged me to write a letter to Nick. Then she asked me to look at the themes that ran through it, like the ones that were also present in my young life.

(As you read through, what unfolds may or may not surprise you. Perhaps it will even bring up some parallels from your own journey.)

The letters that poured out went like this (portions shared are completely unedited):

Dear Nick,

I hate you for not choosing me. I hate you for always running to everyone else when there were issues in our relationship. I hate you for not holding our relationship as something sacred. I hate you for always worrying about pleasing everyone else. I hate you for not facing your demons. I hate you for not forgiving me. I hate you for not defending me for not putting our family, me, our daughters first. I hate you for being weak. I hate you for hurting me. I hate you for lying.

I hate you for your anger and your depression. I hate you for making us feel like we were never enough for you. I hate you for always needing to be out. For always needing more, for never being satisfied. I hate you for caring what other people think.

But as I kept writing, here's what I realized I was actually saying (to my mom):

I hate you for not choosing me. I hate that everyone else was important, not me. I hate that you couldn't acknowledge the truth of what was happening. I hate that you

*blamed me. I hate that you didn't protect me. I hate
that you didn't love yourself enough to know you deserve
better. I hate you for minimizing my experiences. I hate
that you were never home. I hate that you cared what
other people thought. I hate that I was not enough for you
to love. I hate that it was easier to blame me and to turn a
blind eye to doing the work of fixing the situation. I hate
that I grew up alone. I hate that I hate you and dad and
then I get judged for that hate. I hate that you put your
own needs before my own.*

Have you ever tried doing something like this? Change
the name of the person in your current life that you feel is
the bane of your existence, that you're so sure is the root of all
your misery, and then replace it with someone in your past—
namely your parents. Does it fit? Crazy, I know. So much of
the anger I poured into our relationship was a direct result of
my childhood. Did I have reasons to be angry with him too,
of course—but we sure do have a way of recreating what we
are unconsciously trying to heal—yes, you are that powerful!
Also most of the hatred we project onto others is truly our own
self hatred because of what we were taught. Heal yourself, heal
your relationship patterns.

I'd like to think that there was no other time but now
where I was truly capable of not just facing the trauma but
feeling it in my body. It leaked out here and there over the
years. I started feeling pangs of anxiety at the beginning of my
divorce. I felt it every time we went to court. When I would
get pulled over by a police officer, regardless of how tiny the
infraction. When I got evicted. Whenever it seemed someone
was mad at me. In fact, it was there all along but it became

monumental. I couldn't ignore it. I tried very hard to keep up with my everyday life. And I have to say, despite the fact that I was living in what felt like a 24-7 panic nightmare, I somehow managed to live my life pretending everything was fine. Not that this is necessarily a good thing. I went to work as often as I could (although I lived in a constant state of "I'm dying"). I tried so hard being a consistent mom, but so many days were spent going to bed early, praying for a different outcome come the morning.

I don't know how I did it but I did, and I did it with the help and support of countless people.

Severed Ties

As I started to feel better. I began dating again. This was not allowed, as it turned out. I was always in Nick's family's good graces as long as I did what I was supposed to do. I was allowed to live in my own home only if I was single. The minute Nick found out I was dating again—all hell broke loose. Saying he was angry was an understatement. He was irate, livid. He felt triggered and betrayed in the deepest way. And on the outside, you might wonder why was he so angry? We were not together. And we weren't—but there was also always so much ambiguity in our lives. No boundaries, right? No clear delineations of this is okay and this isn't.

However, in my mind, we broke up for good December 2018. There was never anything remotely intimate going on with us for quite some time. We no longer lived together yet he was very much still a part of my life. We owned a home together, and while he didn't live there, he came over quite often especially during the pandemic when life came to a standstill and there was not much else to do. He bought us all bikes. We went for bike rides. He came over for dinner. I was taking care of his dogs and his father while he did his own thing. It was temporary, this arrangement in my opinion, but clearly to him, it left this hope that somehow, someway, we would make it work. While I had really promised myself there was no turning back on New Year's Eve, obviously he did not.

Although I lived in our home alone with our daughters, he still had the keys. He never came over unannounced—but now that he was angry, that changed. And all of this was a result of *me* not wanting to establish clear boundaries so that I wouldn't rock the boat and no one would be upset with me—especially him. The situation forced me into setting those boundaries in a concrete way for the first time in my life and in our relationship. You can imagine how well that went over. People who don't like you setting boundaries are those that have benefitted from your wishy-washy nature. And it wasn't just because I had a boyfriend, although in hindsight the boyfriend's role in my life was equal parts miniscule and profound because he was such a clear representation of "Carmin, as much as you say you are divorced, broken up, etc. It's very messy." I mean he actually said those words to me and again sometimes I just couldn't really see things until they were this glaringly obvious.

We don't stay in unhealthy relationships with no benefits. *Both* parties are always benefitting somehow and most of the time it's because of comfort, familiarity, a fear of moving on, a fear of the unknown, or a fear of letting go and finally saying this is impossible! Nick and I's arrangement wasn't the result of two people who were sure they did not want to be together, were able to co-parent, be friends, and be happy for each other in new relationships. It was two people who had no boundaries, not making clear cut decisions, afraid to really move on.

I ended up involving law enforcement over a domestic dispute because I did not know what else to do and Nick and I would never have a peaceful relationship in any capacity again. Life will remove you from where you don't belong. If you do not sever those ties, life will force you into it and if you wait too long, it won't be pretty. This part *is* unfortunate because when you have children they are the ones who are impacted the most.

Your Body Remembers Everything

Life will continue to push you towards healing and get louder the more you ignore it. Before we severed ties I was involved in a car accident. Luckily, I was traveling solo. A car hit a car that hit a car that hit my car in bumper-to-bumper traffic traveling west on the Southern State Parkway in Long Island. I was car number four. I can't believe how much of an impact I felt. My head jolted forward; my glasses flew off my face. Luckily, I didn't hit anyone in front of me but I was so shaken. I immediately called my friend Joanne who had herself recently gotten into an accident. From someone who had studied traumatic brain injury in college, I knew how jagged the inside of my skull is and I was worried about internal damage. She told me to go to another community healer, Adam. He is a physical therapist and a craniosacral therapist—but honestly so much more than that.

I was feeling so much better by now. I was no longer living in a constant state of drain and fear. However, I still had physical effects from processing old pain. The main thing was the numbness on the left side of my body. To say Adam is incredible is an understatement. I felt so safe and at ease during our sessions, which allowed me to leave so much on that table. He incorporated his specific brand of magic, just like all the other amazing people I felt led to prior.

After a few sessions with him, I was led to chiropractic work. Adam recommended a colleague named John. The chiropractor was something I feared because my mom went as a kid and just felt frightened to me watching her and hearing the cracking, but nevertheless I felt called to the next step.

It was as if the physical impact of the car was inviting me to visit not just the pain of the impact but all the other pain that was stored underneath. John found stiffness, tightness, knots upon knots that I never actually felt until he brought it to my attention! In my shoulders, my back, my hips. I was like, "Wow, have I really been living with all this pain and was just disconnected from it?" I knew it was not just from the accident.

Their work brought me back to my body in yet another deeper way. While John wasn't trauma informed, the first session released so much for me. The only thing I needed was a box of tissues. I just kept crying. Our body is always looking for a release. If you have any sort of blockage or you feel stuck, it will get trapped in your very cells in your tissue, and body work is truly a beautiful way to go.

Dissolving Connections

The last connection Nick and I had aside from our babies was our blue house on the corner. It was filled with what felt like more bad memories than good. But I loved her. I was grateful to her and to Nick. Some people asked why I didn't force the sale of the home when we were first divorced like we agreed to, but a part of me was always afraid to really move on, to cut ties and let go, and setting boundaries with him was always hard. I also didn't want the fight. I had subconsciously learned my whole life to remain silent as to not ruffle any feathers and I knew selling the house was something he did not want. I was in no position to have yet another legal battle. Nick also represented the only home or family I ever knew, and even though in many ways it appeared better than where I came from, it was still unhealthy.

After listening to a life changing workshop on the power of Feng Shui on the way home from one of our many road trips, I began to clean, organize, and purge. I removed the last remnants of Nick's belongings from our home. I removed the extra dressers that I purchased for him. I removed his suits from my closet. I cleaned my home. I removed the privacy film he placed over our front and back doors when he was in a relationship with someone else. I cleared the space. I burnt sage. I cried. I felt the presence of Our Lady, and the energy of our home weeping and wanting to be cleansed.

Death and Clearing

I was still doing so much clearing, and I hired someone to paint. I, for the first time, made this space solely my own. Then something strange happened. I am sure it was a complete coincidence but still felt so powerful in its own right. All the men in the space that I lived in made their way out—completely out. Nick, although not living there for a while, stopped coming around due to a court order in place—talk about a huge boundary set.

Both my ex-father-in-law, who still lived downstairs from the girls and me, and our upstairs neighbor—a single man named Alex—passed away within a few weeks of one another. For the first time ever, the girls lived in our blue cape on the corner completely alone. It was so eerie to say the least.

Although Nick and I were no longer on speaking terms, I was still caring for his dad, but when we severed ties, his dad cut me off too. I was beyond hurt after all I had done for him—but that's how the blind loyalty worked in that family.

The girls lost their grandfather, and I lost a man who for twenty-two years was like a father to me. And Nick and I lost another bond between us. Even though his dad no longer spoke to me, certain things were unavoidable living in the same house together. Although we did not always agree on things—there was a love there, and we shared a lot of good memories and laughter. I find some solace that as circumstances would have it, he did apologize to me before he passed.

His dad and I did a lot of things together. He always said I was like a daughter to him, and I really took the role of being his caregiver. He too had a difficult time with boundaries. He was one of those people who would text and call a thousand times in a row if he needed something and you didn't answer. Interestingly enough, we had a lot in common. He loved thrifting and garage sales, and he loved hearing about my finds and knowing about and even sitting in on my do-it-yourself projects. He always watched my Facebook lives and wanted to hear all about *Lessons For My Daughters* happenings. He would always encourage me to further my education or expand my business. When it came to the girls, he was always there for every special occasion and milestone, and he loved just being a part of the everyday stuff. He would come up the stairs a thousand times a day just to sit outside with the girls and me if we were coming up. He was quite the character, and everyone on the block knew him.

Although he left our home a few months prior to go to the hospital, it never felt quite as empty as it did when the day came knowing with certainty that he was never coming back.

Transforming My Relationship to the Masculine

With no physical men around, one of the most powerful things I had to do on the next leg of my journey was to really heal my relationship to the masculine. After I began feeling like myself again, I knew I had to rewrite the story I had about men. The lens I filtered them through had so much to do with my early childhood experiences.

Clearly, I didn't have much to go on in terms of male role models. In fact, one of the most concrete lessons my mother taught me—if you remember—was never to depend on a man. She showed me that in her actions, but she also spoke those words specifically to me. My mother didn't say much, so when she said something to me, anything, I hung on to it like gospel.

She was the sole provider and bread winner, and I spent most of my life in fear that I would lose her. Even though she was not available to me truly, in any of the ways that I needed her, still she represented this false sense of security to me.

There was some sort of predictability with her. Every day I would walk to Nonna's house after school and call her at the factory she worked in and they would call out to her to come to the phone. And that was our routine—the phone call after school and waiting patiently for her to get back home from work so I would not have to be alone with my father.

Any deviation from that schedule sent me into a panic. She had no idea. She was oblivious to me and my needs in so many ways, as she remains to this day. And then of course, there was my father, who was clearly mentally ill (we will go with that story to make any sort of sense of his behaviors and actions, because one would have to be quite sick to do the things he did). Since I could not depend on him in any way, he just solidified my mother's lesson.

So, it was clear—my life was pretty fucked up from the start. I took those experiences and desperately searched for love anywhere I could find it. I re-created a lot of the same situations. My mother told me never to depend on a man so I became wildly independent. I was successful in all the ways that a "boss bitch" should be, but not in the way that I find now really matters.

You know, people think because I focus on female empowerment (and maybe I am transitioning into a better word for it) that I identify with being a feminist, but I feel like sometimes we get swept up in the cool and trendy thing to do or get caught up in the labels. To me, a lot of modern feminism has turned into man hating, but, news flash, men need women and women need men. Modern ideas are great. It's wonderful to be progressive and not stuck on outdated thinking, but there are also some beautiful traditions, like being in a harmonious relationship that's balanced (but not that *balanced* necessarily means *equal*), that still hold value in the world.

In my opinion, men and women were never meant to be equal. Sure, equal pay for the same job well done, of course, but men and women are different in the most beautiful ways. The energies are meant to balance each other out. There's a reason why men were traditionally hunters and women traditionally stayed behind and raised the children. Not that women never went out on the kill because this is not true but they each put their strengths to the best use. Which is what people still do in societies, companies, and teams. Men are generally more logical, women more intuitive. Of course, there are variations on an incredibly diverse spectrum, but let's not throw biology away completely.

I share all this to say that I have had to unlearn so much conditioning, not only from my mother's unfortunate experience with a man but also with what society keeps spewing out. Yeah, it's definitely great for women to find their way into the workplace, follow their passions, and stand up for reproductive rights. But at the same time there's this undertone of pitting men against women and vice versa that happens everywhere.

All this "I don't need a man" rhetoric and "women ain't loyal" ideologies begins to break society down in a bigger way. More and more single-parent households where women are no longer depending on their man to provide but are now reliant on the government . . . but without getting political and even more long winded, my point is men have it hard too.

They are consistently being told that their only value comes from the salary they earn, the car they drive, their ability to provide, and so on. Told to be strong, keep pushing through, don't show your feelings, take care of everything, and so on. And as I have been out there really dating for the first time in my life—truly dating—I realize so many men are walking around hurt by women, some by this woman in particular.

And that's a big realization coming from me because I spent the greater part of my life dwelling on how men suck and could not be trusted let alone depended on. From my father, to my brother, to my partners. I never looked at how my trauma then caused trauma for all the other men in my life who truly didn't cause me any harm (initially).

So, in working hard to change the way I view men, I have a newfound appreciation for them. Since I now appreciate them, they show up completely differently to me. And this is just the way the world works with ANYTHING. Your outer world is a reflection of your inner world, period. Your beliefs about the world directly influence the experiences you have. That's not to say we won't meet a total jerk just because—of course that's a possibility—but having a knowledge that our inside helps to shape what we see on the outside is huge. And making the conscious effort to shift the deep down, stuck, limiting beliefs first takes awareness and then great courage. Doing the work is not for the meek, but it is always soooo worth it.

I meet beautiful men everywhere I go now—of all ages. Men wanting to do things for me, men who are thoughtful. Men who smile, want to have conversations, hold doors, give me their number, propose, and so on. Men who tell me I am inspiring them to be better versions of themselves.

I'll give you the sweetest example of what is truly deep down in a man's heart that he probably keeps so buried. I have a client—he's four. During one of our sessions, I told him my favorite color was green. A few sessions later we were coloring. He told me to take the green marker because it was my favorite. How thoughtful and sweet that he even remembered? Men are all beautiful. They start off innocent just like the rest of us and the world hardens them up. I love to believe in a world where my father was beautiful and innocent once too.

The goal in life is to take off that armor—go back to that childlike innocence and to find the safe people to surround yourself with where you CAN do that. Look around and appreciate one another. We are taught to be rivals on so many levels but when working together, kingdoms are made. It may seem idealistic or even simplistic, but I invite you to drop your biases and past hurts and watch a new world open up to you. So, if you have a beautiful man in your life, thank him today.

A Summer of Synchronicities

Happiness and peace, worthiness and the feeling of being deserving, is always, always an inside job now that you are an adult. The healing can only ever happen within, and then it gets reflected outside of us. The longer we try to search for that healing outside of ourselves in things and in others, the deeper the pain becomes.

Not to say that we don't need others. We most definitely do. If we are brave enough to face our own pain, we will see that the pain that gets triggered through relating with others can be used as a tool to transmute it. Our reactions are a BIG clue, and if we believe it is a gift—a light shining on the areas where we need healing—then we will use it to our advantage and come out stronger on the other side. But this journey is not for the faint of heart and neither is that of love.

And so with this new information I went on a very different dating journey, it was wildly wonderful to let go and let myself truly be held and supported (although scary as fuck—really saying goodbye to my hyper-independence). Never underestimate the power of being seen and loved.

Life is one big synchronicity if you pay attention. For one summer in particular there was no shortage of magic. I felt like life took me by the hand and effortlessly led me from one step to the next while simultaneously highlighting my power to create outcomes with my thoughts and my intentions. You are always being reminded how miraculous life is when you are mindful of that fact and if you think back on your own life you will find many examples of this. I love my life so much now, and noticing how it is always in alignment is what keeps me going. If life doesn't feel like MAGIC to you every day—I promise you—it is POSSIBLE.

My youngest daughter loves to watch TV shows—not movies, shows. The more seasons, the better. It's a way for us to connect. We find a mutually agreeable series to watch, and then we spend some time each week getting together to see it all the way through. At one particular time, it was difficult to find something that was age appropriate because so much today contains content that is too heavy, dark, or sexual. I took her back to my youth and asked her if she would consider *Dawson's Creek*. To my surprise she said yes and over the course of a year we got through six seasons.

While watching the show I was drawn to these characters in a different way than I did as a kid, and I was also drawn to the cast—who these actors were and what became of them. Still processing so much of what I had gone through, I really fell in love with the character of Pacey played by Joshua Jackson. He was the troubled kid, the black sheep much like myself. I also was drawn to his representation of the masculine. The way he had such a big heart and how he did anything for the girl he loved. Pacey was a fierce protector—something I had always wished I had in my own life.

I also love to travel and take road trips, so after our journey of watching the show, I took my girl to visit the filming locations in Wilmington, North Carolina. In the midst of planning this surprise for her, I somehow came upon an article with this exact information written by a writer for *Oprah Daily*. She encouraged readers to reach out to her and I did. She personally gave me the inside scoop of all the filming locations to check out. It was so cool to have lunch with her in the restaurant Pacey "owns" at the conclusion of the series!

Around this time, I also began following Joshua Jackson's career and watched a lot of his other shows and interviews he had done. I took a big interest in his work and who he is as a person. I found him to be a pretty incredible human (from the little I know, obviously), but a lot can be said about someone based on the way they use their fame and how that translates into what they put into the world. He is clearly intentional with his work and the roles he takes on, and I became a big fan.

He's done some incredible things like: being a part of making *The Laramie Project* (the story of Michael Shepard), he played in *When They See Us* (the documentary about the Central Park 5). He also took on the leading role in *Children of a Lesser God* on Broadway, and the way he spoke of his experience in working alongside someone who is deaf was really beautiful. His humanness and open heartedness truly comes through in so much of the work he involves himself with. I absolutely loved his character in *The Affair* on Showtime—but I also loved a lot of everything the series touched upon. It was so healing for me in many ways. If you have ever had the experience of how a work of art can touch you in such a profound way, you will understand.

I put an intention into the world that I wanted to meet him. Not too long after that, I found myself on a Zoom call with the actor who played the other main character on the show, Dawson (James Van Der Beek) and not too long after that, I was indeed sitting in the front row of the Tribeca Film Festival just a few feet away from where Joshua Jackson himself was speaking about his role in his then series—*Dr. Death*. It was incredible to be a part of this culturally iconic NYC thing. (If you don't know how the Tribeca Film Festival got its start— look into it.)

When I first heard the title of this new show, I thought, "Hmmm, this isn't my thing, but what are the chances that this man whose work I have been so completely enthralled by is in my own backyard?" I had to be there. Funnily enough, I almost didn't make it because I was flying home from a vacation in Mexico, and we got stuck there an extra night. But I was meant to be there. I made it. I stayed even through the rain to be a few feet from him!

Joshua had the lead role in a show based on a real doctor who maimed and killed his patients—intentionally called Dr. Death. I didn't think I could be interested, but it turns out it was about a CORRUPT medical system that covers up horrific things even though they know the truth! How coincidental? It reminded me of my own life in many ways: so many people chose to cover up instead of standing up for the victims. The show is really about the brave doctors who stood up to the system.

Medical malpractice is the third leading cause of death, believe it or not. The series advocates for people being aware of patient rights. What an important conversation, especially at a time when we were in the height of the pandemic.

While I was watching *The Affair*, I took an interest in its filming location, which was actually located about 100 miles east of where I live in the picturesque town of Montauk, Long Island—known simply as "the end." I felt very pulled to learn more about and visit the area. This then serendipitously led me to an Instagram ad asking for volunteers for the Montauk Film Festival. I knew I was meant to be there, so I signed up. A lot of volunteers were staying out there the whole week, but as it was a two-hour drive for me, I commuted back and forth and volunteered for just some of the days.

One particular day I had plans to volunteer for one thing and at the last minute they completely changed the itinerary because of poor weather conditions but from that moment on, everything went positively right. I got to eat lunch at a place I have been meaning to get to—LUNCH aka Lobster Roll (best lobster roll ever, FYI)—a very big filming location for the show *The Affair*. This amazing woman waited on me, and then proceeded to give me a tour. I got to sit in the very booth where the actors sat, which coincidentally was completely closed off to the public that day!

After that I took part in the behind the scenes filming of an incredibly important panel event on how to preserve the precious groundwater on Long Island. You know while we sit here and frivolously poison the earth, there are people working hard to reverse our callous mistakes? It was so inspiring! I also met an awesome producer there who, guess what? Is ALL ABOUT empowering girls.

I connected with the brilliant people behind the Montauk Film Festival, and I had amazing food and laughs at a restaurant known to have the best view of the sunset on the entire island. Many people I met that day said we wouldn't get to experience one that evening because it was too cloudy and there were many storms on the horizon—but I also had the belief that I would! I went on to witness the most breathtaking sunset that evening, which is proof that your belief in something can literally outshine logic! This also eventually landed me in what literally felt like a scene in *Dawson's Creek* the following day— being kissed on the pier following a delicious dinner. It was a real "pinch me" moment.

The Affair was largely centered around the main character's trauma. It felt so relatable, and I oddly felt very seen and acknowledged through this art. Perhaps the most beautiful thing that came from this experience was how it motivated me to write. One of the other characters on the show was a writer, and he writes about the story of his life. That idea inspired me to finally write this book!

I really have a newfound respect for writers and performers. Taking a story and bringing it to life is no easy feat, but I also admire it when someone takes their life and makes it mean something. Choosing work that really has a purpose. Being intentional with what we put out in the world. I hope I have done a good job of living in this way.

People will tell you that you are living life wrong. You're too this or you're too that. Forget all of that. Let life grab you by the hand and lead you to exactly where you are meant to be every damn time.

Believe in magic again. Notice the serendipity and synchronicity. Is life hard sometimes? Fuck yes! But it is also beautiful, and yes, you are that powerful. Create a life you love now!

On Healthy Love

So, with that, let me tell you about my beloved Thomas. Someone I met during this particularly magical summer. I never thought our relationship would turn into more than being a yes to a fun time. I was so focused on saying yes to all the beautiful opportunities, I wasn't really thinking about the long term, but even when I did, I really never pictured it to be him.

Thomas is a beautiful healer. I knew from pretty early on that he was something to be treasured. He made me feel free to be exactly who I am in every possible way. He witnessed me in the fullest expression of all aspects of me including my sexuality. Without judgment, without intimidation, without jealousy. That in itself was so healing. It was fun, it was easy, but . . . with the depth of being seen and witnessed so deeply, it was inevitable that the trigger would also come.

I was intensely nauseous after one particular interaction with him. It felt like something in the deep dark wells of my being needed purging. I reached out to my somatic therapist, Alycia. It is so important to reach out for help when we need it. During the session, I kept saying "I need to spit" as gross as that may seem. Alycia always taught me not to stop what was ever coming up for me. A yawn, a sigh, a scream, a burp, a runny nose, whatever it was—let it emerge. I felt the urge to spit, which eventually led to vomiting, which was an incredibly needed and beautiful release. While it sounds disgusting, it is so much better for the energy of those feelings, emotions, past trauma to live outside your body than in. How many times do we hold back tears, anger? All energy needs to be released— in a healthy way. I find it interesting that we're always ingesting things like alcohol and drugs or turning to any outlet for escape in a futile attempt to feel happier and free when we're only clogging our systems even more. If it wants to come up, let it. I think the fear of facing certain aspects of ourselves is usually scarier than actually dealing with it. It takes 90 seconds to feel and process an emotion; however, as humans we attach that to so much living inside us from the past that we get stuck in our thinking mind. The body holds all the keys to healing— feel it and let it go.

So, as amazing as Thomas is and was, there was still much work to do. I did a similar dance—he pursued and I pulled away. He was certain he wanted to be with me, and again it scared me to no end. I tried to find every reason we could not be together. I broke things off several times, but he made it clear that he was not going anywhere.

It's been really amazing though to be with a person who not only does not give up but also takes accountability and does the work towards his own healing and towards cocreating the same dream. It has also been incredible to own my sexuality and embrace it, seeing it as a source of my own fulfillment. For so long, I was punished for it and it feels safe to be with someone who doesn't punish me for it nor shame me. My innocence was taken away from me at a really young age and I was used as a tool for someone else's pleasure. It feels really empowering to be that for myself now. I love how in my body I am, how I feel this body as a source of enjoyment and bliss, an incredibly beautiful vehicle in which to navigate the world with. But there is nothing more beautiful than someone who wants to know who you are underneath the surface. Why don't we get to know each other there more deeply, more frequently?

Because, contrastingly, even though we all want to be seen, this is also the scariest thing, the most vulnerable place to be. It's so much easier to be with someone on a solely physical level but to really reveal ourselves? To show another our scars, our trauma—there lies one of the greatest gifts—one of the most powerful healers. To be witnessed without judgment.

Being seen is one of the most powerful gifts we can give one another. Yet more proof that healing cannot be done alone. Sure, you can have some transformative experience off in the mountains of Tibet somewhere, becoming enlightened through meditation. Messages from God, source, the universe—surely occur when we are silent enough to listen. But being in relation to others, there lies the real test.

It reminds me of a Ram Dass quote: "If you think you're enlightened, go spend a week with your family." The people we are closest to obviously trigger us the most, and nothing brings up more than being in an intimate relationship.

Don't underestimate the power of love, of monogamy, of giving yourself to someone else. Giving your heart to someone, trusting them with it, experiencing true vulnerability. Letting someone see the raw nakedness of who you are outside of sex and the bedroom. To love is life's greatest adventure, but to truly be seen—that takes courage.

To take accountability for your feelings, for your wounds, to cultivate a true sense of mutual respect. To communicate without yelling, without insults, with the willingness to really understand the other person. To speak and see with clarity. To see them for who they are, not through the filter of our wounds.

I know who I am now—I know where I end and another person begins. There's a clear boundary, a delineation. That hasn't been easy for someone who was so codependent.

Feeling genuine care for another person. To hold them and the relationship sacred, this was also challenging. I grew up in survival mode, and I could not think of anyone but myself. Therefore, I had a hard time developing genuine compassion and empathy for others.

My relationship with Thomas brought up all my issues with attachment. The closer we got, the more I wanted to pull away. If ever I felt hurt, I wanted to hurt back but one hundred times worse.

The only difference was his love. His presence was unwavering. Even more than that, he never took my feelings personally. He knew my reluctance had nothing to do with him. He knew about my past. He never saw me as broken. He only always saw me as strong and powerful and resilient. He saw me for who I was, and I saw him. This beautiful, powerful, genuine, loyal bright light—so full of love and so full of joy and just a willingness to have fun.

My big feelings never scared him. He willingly sat with them, listened, and never thought I was crazy (or if he did, he never let that show). He was unfazed by where I came from because he could so clearly see where I was going and he wanted to be a part of that. Not be a part of it in a "jump into my bandwagon" kind of way, but more of standing boldly beside me, wanting to be that grounding force. My partner, my safety, my king. For once in my life, I felt safe in the arms of a man.

Being in my power led me to that and led me to believe I was deserving of love. Seeing the love I had poured into myself over the years be reflected back to me tenfold in all ways in all areas, in all directions. What happens when you make peace with your past, honor your inner child, step into who you really are and own your power?

Well, you know it's not an easy feat. The journey has bumps, and you will weave in and out of this place. But you will at last finally arrive in a soft, pillowy space to land. It reminds me of cloud-like Care-a-Lot, where the Care Bears live. Here you will find a sense of peace, calm, true faith, and trust in yourself. You will feel grounded and powerful.

You will feel connected and safe. Knowing that where you are is home and being able to be where you are and being okay with it. Feeling safe in the unknown. Forgiving yourself, your process, your journey (I'm still working on this one). Being more open to giving and receiving love. The ability to be open and vulnerable when appropriate. You will feel anchored into the essence of who you are here on Earth but also clearly connected to a source and all that is (whatever you believe in—even if it's nothing—acknowledging you are a miracle). Content but also knowing that life happens. You can roll with it. You are your own center. Remember; you are the thermostat, no longer the thermometer.

Coming Full Circle

Over the years, *Lessons For My Daughters* has expanded into many courses and workshops that have been taught to girls all over the world and more recently inclusive of boys too.

Since its inception, my organization and I have had articles written about us, gotten the attention of print media, podcasts, television, politicians, and has even been recognized through awards. And although I have taught girls across states and continents, nothing has given me greater joy than to bring hope back to where I came from.

I have had the honor of teaching my programs at not only the high school I graduated from but also the junior high school I attended, Intermediate School 93 and Grover Cleveland High School, respectively. And I did this with the help of a longtime friend and former classmate, Nancy, who is now the vice president of a local bank in our community—Ridgewood Savings Bank. With Nancy's belief in my vision, we acquired 100 percent funding for various schools and programs throughout New York City. I was later asked to return to be the keynote speaker at my high school's graduation ceremony: twenty-three years after sitting in those same auditorium seats myself, this time with my daughters in the audience! It is really so incredible what you can create when you follow that internal guidance and trust the calling of your heart. There is really nothing you can't do.

As the years went on, more and more women (many of them moms) were called to my work. Over and over, they would ask if I could teach them the same classes I was teaching girls. It really made me realize that so many of us were still walking around needing those same reminders, wanting to polish up the skills that maybe they forgot or, like me, never learned. Even though that made sense because I was one of those people, I was in awe that adults found value in what I was creating. I taught a class on cultivating healthy boundaries for teens, and a mom showed up to my class. She registered for her daughter but it was she who logged into the Zoom that day and she had so many questions. I put my self-doubt aside, got out of my own way, and put together that same class for women. Not only were women signing up, but I also had the largest enrollment than any of my other courses—in the height of a global pandemic no less! Women showed up for themselves, both in person and online, many who I knew and respected. It was a huge validation on how much this work is needed.

As I have evolved as a human, woman, and student of life, I continue to be called to teach what I learn and more specifically what I have managed to overcome. If you would have asked a young me what I would love to do as an adult, it would have always been to help others overcome childhood sexual trauma. However, I never, ever thought I would be able to hold that tender and raw space for others when I was in so much pain myself. But life has a way of allowing things to unfold in its own right timeline.

I dug in and I knew I needed to create a program specifically for women, for mothers. I began interviewing women, many whom I knew and some who I didn't, and I asked them what their biggest struggle was, and I saw the patterns emerge. Interview after interview, many of the moms were sharing the same things. They wanted to find balance between their work, their relationships, and their role as a mother. Almost everyone mentioned they wish they had more time in the day. So many shared that they felt a calling to do something more, but they had no idea how to fit it in or even more so where to start. That was when *Embodiment: 45 Days to Peace + Pleasure + Grace* came to fruition. It was born after compiling all the information from the brave and candid women sharing what they were struggling with coupled with some of the most powerful tools I had learned over the years to help facilitate my own healing and growth—my ability to thrive and no longer just survive.

It's centered around using the power of connecting back to yourself to live in alignment with your purpose while feeling grounded into peace. Which consequently doesn't mean life will never be turbulent, but that you become a lot more unshakeable. Teaching you to fully enjoy pleasure in all aspects of your life, while simultaneously giving yourself permission for grace—the knowing that it will never be and should not have to be and look perfect. Its purpose is to find your balance, to live from your center (which is love), so as to not pass on the faulty lessons you may have learned growing up and put them onto your own children. It's about having the courage to break the patterns in your life that are no longer serving you so you can truly be free to live the life you envision for both yourself and your family without that gnawing feeling of being stuck.

At first, many of the women I interviewed were those who were part of that first cohort, but as the business model expanded, I ended up writing a specific ad for the kind of mother I was wanting to help. The beautiful thing was when I was asked to think of my ideal client, it was the same as when I was asked who I was speaking to with my book. I so much wanted to help moms who were like me. They were clear that they experienced trauma, and they were even clearer that they did not want to pass that trauma on to their children. But even with the intention of being better, they felt the unconscious patterning emerging and spilling out to the people they loved the most. There was a time I never thought I could hold that raw and tender space for women standing in a place I once was. I am here now and truly in awe that life can come full circle. I am doing the work that so long ago I knew I was meant to do, and I just want to remind you that it is possible for you too. So many of the moms I speak to also want to take their pain and transmute their experience in a way to heal others. They remind me so very much that I am not alone, that healing is possible and that there is so much more good than bad in the world. They have a drive to end the cycle of trauma. Eventually it will be done once and for all.

Following the Light of the Sun

If there was one thing that I always envisioned for my life, it was to live by the water. My deepest desire was to live by the ocean, but I never really believed that was a possibility. I had a taste of the dream briefly in Nyack, even though it was the river not the ocean. I somehow internalized it wasn't meant for me when I felt like it was all being ripped out from under me. Also, houses on the beach historically can be the most expensive real estate, especially on certain parts of Long Island. There was a tiny part of me that believed it would not be possible, yet year after year I always put it on my vision board. What I taught my clients to do, I did with them and I did for myself.

As my relationship with Thomas progressed, we talked about moving in together. In fact, one of the things we immediately found we had in common was that we both wanted to find a home on the water by the following summer. When we first started looking into buying a home, I fell in love with this beautiful place on Shore Drive in a town named Merrick. I even loved the address—this is just as important as the location to me. I wanted it to *scream* water! The home was so beautiful on the outside. It was completely white with blue accents (of course)—Nonna was always with me, and I thought this house in particular was meant for us. I began getting signs from Stella Maris, also known as Our Lady Star of the Sea. I printed a picture of her and placed it in the window of my current home. Shore Drive did not pan out the way we planned. At first I felt so defeated because I really thought that was the one, but reminding myself to trust, we began looking in a neighborhood called Long Beach.

If you recall, Long Beach had been calling me for quite some time. We began working with a different realtor who was so on top of it. Her name was Mary—of course. We only saw a few before we fell in love with a magnificent blue house on the corner! And the address? Beech Street! We immediately said yes, but there were a few financial hurdles to overcome. Thomas and I agreed to be completely honest about our respective situations in our application. That way if we got it, we knew it was truly meant to be. And here we are! And one of the most incredible, incredible parts is that you can see the ocean and the boardwalk, the ships, the runners going by all from our balcony. It is a literal dream come true, one that has been such a long time coming.

What a beautiful reminder to really trust not only the timing of your life but to see that you are truly being led. Just as the butterfly is led by the light of the sun, so are we—and for me, the Divine light of the mother. There's a peace within me now that I have never known and so it would make sense that my home would reflect that. Our home is so light, airy, calm, and spacious. We've started over completely anew and have handpicked every single piece of furniture and decor. We live not far from a church—St. Mary of the Isle—and believe it or not, Long Beach has been dubbed the "city by the sea." I know Stella Maris Star of the Sea has brought us here.

I manifested the beach house . . . finally! I still pinch myself. And remember the Feng Shui woman who inspired me so much? The woman who helped me clear the energy of my first home, Kate. We hired her and she's helping us balance the energy here by placing items in the space according to Feng Shui principles. It feels so amazing to decorate our home with the intention of all that we want to create here.

It is also a big reminder to truly be cautious of what you wish for. Thomas and I have always been called to the water, and water is a powerful thing, especially the energy of the ocean. It has a way of flushing out exactly what does not belong. In fact, not too long after moving here and taking on a new big financial responsibility, I lost my job as a speech language pathologist for good. It was scary to let go of another safety net, yet life was forcing me again to something I kept holding on to in fear of really taking the next step.

Even though *Lessons For My Daughters* is thriving and growing more every day and in my heart I know this is what I am meant to be doing, it was beyond frightening. But if you want the new life, you have to be willing to let go of the old, no matter how scary it feels. Also, you do deserve the life of your dreams. If it is calling to you, it is indeed possible, so keep that faith.

But as beautiful, flowery, and passionate as our Leo-Libra love has been moving into the same space has shed a light on all of the parts of ourselves we did not even know we continued to keep hidden! All of the shadows have come out and I mean ALL. It has been such a powerful teacher and healer although not always comfortable at all, in fact at times quite painful.

More Letting Go

In moving from one blue house on the corner to another (could that be any more symbolic) another tie was inevitably broken. I finally gave Nick his dogs back—Gia and Bailey. When we merged as a couple a second time, we merged pets, and I became a dog mama to these two beautiful and distinct personalities. G is a snowy white, sweetheart of a Pitbull-terrier mix, and Bea is a thin, lanky, protective, goofy and ever-so-loving German Shepard. I am so blessed to have had them in my life, but I knew they did not belong to me and I already had two cats of my own.

Before I made the permanent move to the beach, we lost our precious cat Oreo. This was so extremely devastating to me. Oreo has been with me since the beginning of this healing journey, and I am so sad he didn't make it to the beach house. All of us really miss him, including his brother Fudge. Fudge has never known life without another fur baby, and it has been really interesting to see a new side of his personality emerge here. He is really thriving as the sole pet of this beautiful three-story home, and I know his big brother watches over him. In fact, as I write this very paragraph, Fudge went from hopping up into the built-in bookcase, the one shelf in particular his brother's remains are on, to coming to sit on my arm while I type this.

Animals are such a great reminder of how energy works. The legal dispute between Nick and I over our former home has finally ended. It was such a strange feeling for so many years of arguing to come to an end in just a day and a half. We will receive a decision soon, and while I am sad it had to go to such extremes and lengths, I know everything happens in divine timing and that will work itself out too. In fact, the decision is set to be given on the nineteen years and one day anniversary of our marriage. I signed my interest in the property over to him and it really felt like a letting go of one life to fully step into the other moment.

Section 5

Adult Butterfly

Turning Your Pain into Your Mission

It took me so long to fully connect back to the core of who I was. The me that Nonna spoke to every time she saw me. This has now become my mission. To help be the bridge that keeps you connected to your own light. The untouchable, unchangeable part of you. I assist in helping women be less afraid of the darkness that too will lead to your eventual transformation.

I promise if you hang around me long enough, I'll have you feeling like you're magical, worthy, powerful, and a reason to celebrate daily. And you know what? That's not something you can fake. That's the result of a lot of unlearning. A lot of chipping away at all that is NOT you. It reminds me of the famous saying by the magnificent Italian Renaissance artist Michelangelo when he said: "I saw the angel in the marble and carved until I set him free."

And guess what? That's your job, and that's my job too. Sometimes we need help along the way. I actually make the bold statement that we *always* need help along the way. Ram Dass also said (I love his quotes): "We're all just walking each other home." Home has taken on a whole new meaning for me, as you can imagine. Home used to be a scary and unsafe place that made me feel so disconnected and unsure of myself. Someone telling you over and over again that what happened to you didn't happen is really going to mess with you. I didn't trust myself, and I went on to make a lot of poor decisions because of it.

Today, home is a state of pure joy where I feel the life flowing through my veins so strongly that I can't ignore it. I can't take it for granted even if I tried. And when you feel this way, you can't help but want to share it. Like the single flame that ignites a million other lights—you want to be that, you want to live that.

This is one of the reasons I never got into drinking or doing drugs. The number one reason was that having the experiences I had, I never wanted to take the chance of being in a situation where I was not one hundred percent in control of my body. The other reason was that in fleeting moments I would feel intense joy, true joy, and I never wanted to do anything that would numb that too. I would feel as though I was high on life just by doing those things that I loved.

Those moments I would later learn were hints and guideposts for healing, shortcuts to coming back to myself. You have that power inside you. You can set the angel free within yourself. If you need help accessing it, that is why I am here. That is the purpose of this book.

Healing Has Always Been There

Other healers may show up in the way of places, actions, or things that draw you in. For me, the three biggest pulls were always the ocean, movement, and writing.

We are nature; therefore, nature is healing to us. We experience life through our human bodies; therefore, bodies are a vehicle for healing as well. You have naturally gravitated to certain things in your whole life that are a respite, a medicine for your soul that has been helping you get back to yourself all along. What calls to you?

The Magic of Water

There's something about the ocean that's always been so healing for me. "Ameliorated by the sea," a friend of mine, Jonathan, always says to me. I'm not sure if it's the mystery or the power, but the ocean holds all of my secrets and all of my prayers. It's a place where my heart has always felt like home. I feel unjudged, accepted. It makes me feel larger than life and completely insignificant, all at the same time. I bring my pain and sadness to the ocean to be washed away. I bring my gratitudes and dreams so that they may be magnified. As I enter her power and grace, I thank life for another myriad breathtaking experiences and, just like the waves, they come and go.

The ocean is a living, breathing, expansive, and powerful thing. A mystery. No one truly knows the depths of its existence. We take for granted the way it magnificently nourishes life. The ocean is so cleansing and mesmerizing that it sounds like a meditation putting you in a trance-like state. Maybe it's because our bodies are largely water with a unique rhythm and vibration that exists from birth until death. When we swim in it, we are encapsulated by water the way we were in the womb. I wonder what it means to be pulled and gravitate to this powerful force of nature. It is like a magical reset button, a recharge and replenishment. To me, the ocean is representative of the mother, and those who feel called to her waters will be renewed once again. I feel so grateful to her for blessing me with her powerful medicine.

What I also love about the ocean and the powerful strength of water is that she can be still or she can rage and be destructive. I see myself in her. She reminds me that it's okay to feel and to stand full in that expression. It's also the perfect place to dream. In fact, one of the positive things I remember from childhood is our trips to the beach. My cousin John and I would dig in the sand until we reached the precious water. It was a ritual for us.

As I got older, the ocean continued to call me. I would take the three long train rides with my friends from my neighborhood to the beach as early as junior high school, and it was always worth it. I am drawn to all the bodies of water. I've been blessed to live in a castle-like home overlooking the beautiful Hudson River, and now I live in a gorgeous three-story home with views of the Atlantic Ocean—a literal dream come true. One of my all-time favorite bodies of water that I have visited so far is the Mediterranean Sea. I wonder if it's because that's where my roots are; however, even a bath makes me feel at peace! Water is a massive conductor of energy, which can be why I always seem to get such clear messages when I am submerged.

Here's a little free write I did where the ocean's magic came to me in the form of words (which is also clearly another healing modality):

Waves crashing on the beach washing over me pulling
me into the night taking me back to the sea running into
the water it's calling me. Here I go for all my troubles,

here I go for all I need. I leave so much here but take so much with me. I think the ocean is my home. I think this is where I am from. I hope one day to return to you for all eternity. I love being encapsulated by your presence. It feels so powerful and strong. Here I am enveloped by your beautiful and magical song. I want to stay in your energy forever. I want to dance under the moonlight. I want to feel this love forever, this song that reminds me of home.

How has Mother Nature served as a respite for you lately? Is there a place or a practice that calls to you that feels like freedom?

Movement Is Vital

Speaking of freedom, another powerful lesson I have learned is that movement is absolutely essential. The thing about growing up in such a tumultuous way is that the really joyful moments actually stand out because they appeared few and far between. One of the best experiences I had with my father was the day he decided to take my brother and I to buy roller skates. I will never quite know what made him do so but I am grateful for this sweet memory. My roller skates were white with blue and red stripes, and my brother's were blue with red and white stripes. We took them for a spin the moment we got home. As soon as he put them on, my brother fell and was adamant about never trying again. As for me, I fell in love (and also fell and scraped my knees hundreds of times but never gave up). Roller skating gave me the sense of freedom that I longed for. As I got older, I grew out of the white skates and right into those blue skates, so they were something that my father did not buy in vain.

When I entered middle school, it was quite a distance from my house and I walked the nine blocks to school alone. I was blessed because adjacent to the school building was a playground. Although the school seemed far from my house, I would still manage to get there early just to go on the swings beforehand. Sometimes my friends would be there, and we would do that thing where one of us sits and the other one stands on the same swing together, pumping higher and higher. Ironically, I've always been afraid of heights (even the seesaw freaks me out sometimes), but something about the swings gave me this sense of being free. Maybe it was the wind in my hair or just something associated with the act of feeling childlike and carefree, which I was robbed of a lot of in my life. Whatever it was, it made me happy. It still does.

As I grew even older, my friends and I started going out to nightclubs. We were then toward the tail end of junior high school, and we began going out to clubs every weekend. One of the most popular places was this Greek spot called Papagalos. We were clearly too young to get in, but there was a benefit to being female and pretty. We managed to somehow never get carded. As we got older, we moved on to clubs in New York City. There were always huge lines to get in, but that didn't deter us. We would get there just when the doors opened and dance all night into the wee morning hours when the club lights came on once again and the place was closing down. The drug ecstasy was popular at the time, which made people really thirsty, so you'd see hundreds of partygoers carrying water bottles. I always had water too but it was just because all I wanted to do was dance, dance, dance all night.

Others always just assumed that I was high, and I was. I was high on the music, the dancing, the movement, the connection to my body. It did send me into deep ecstasy without any need for manufactured substances. Nothing else mattered but me, the music, and the dance floor. It was another thing that made me feel deliciously free.

My friends and I didn't care if the dance floor was empty; we had no problem being the first ones on. We danced atop stages, on speakers—it didn't matter. Those were some of the best times of my life.

Even though I was still very disassociated from my body in my everyday life, in hindsight I realize it was the movement that helped unconsciously move through all that was stored within my cellular memory. The movement kept my body working optimally. As I got older and got into a relationship and all that single life stuff was over, I became more sedentary. That was when I started coming apart at the seams, and that was when I started really feeling all the pain that I carried in my body. Don't get me wrong—it wasn't just because I stopped dancing, but the dancing was unequivocally a tool for healing, processing, shedding, and coming back to myself.

You can't lead a sedentary lifestyle and be healthy. It's impossible. It's not even about weight. It's about the fact that your body and your cells hold onto so much that talking alone can never release it—and I mean *never*. You have to move your body. You have to find a way to connect to the pleasure that exists simply by being alive in your body. You have to connect to the magic and power that runs through your veins, and get rid of the rest of that crap that is literally in the way of you feeling ecstatic every damn day. She demands that of us. Just the way you cleanse in other ways, a shower or a bath, the body needs to be cleansed of the heavy stagnant energy that gets clogged up inside us from both the past and the present.

The days that I indulged the most in releasing that energy (and the movement in no way needs to be rigorous) were the days that I'd be flying so high that I'd literally be giddy to the point that I would pay to hang out with myself. It makes me feel so much like I'm on cloud nine, it actually seems ridiculous to feel that amount of fun by literally doing nothing. To simply be energized by myself and by life.

And this is ground zero. This is the baseline. I truly believe that. All the trauma and beliefs we end up taking on as a result of said trauma gets caked on like the clouds covering the sun on a stormy day. Your light is always there. Don't ever forget that. This too shall pass, so do not give up. People chasing the high outside of themselves know what they're trying to get back to, but they are looking externally instead of internally. You are the drug. Find your way back to it.

Move pain out of the way to revel in joy. Your body is a vehicle for joy. Quite simply, love her, honor her, and support her in feeling her best. Joy never leaves you. It's always underneath. Movement is essential. Get up and dance!

Trust Your "Mistakes"

I wish I could tell you that healing is a linear path. I wish I could spell out the recipe and take you from A to B without any interruption. But the truth is healing can be painful and it's almost always messy. It is a start and stop over and over type of thing. It is a feeling of taking two steps forward and twenty-seven steps back.

I'm older and I'm wiser now, and I know that you can never truly go backward, even though it absolutely does feel that way. Because it seems as though you are repeating the same patterns, making the same mistakes, doing the same thing over and over, thinking that somehow, some way, something is going to be different. But the truth is healing is more like a spiral. Sometimes you have to revisit certain experiences more than one time, only in a deeper way, and sometimes it feels like an over and over again thing that makes you want to bang your head against the wall because you can't seem to just get it. But you can and you are. As I've said before, I have learned that the journey of life is an unlearning of all the untruths you've picked up along the way.

I can't tell you how grateful I am for all the people who supported me over the years. I must've told the same stories a thousand times over. I felt like I was reliving the same experiences time and again. And it really did seem like that at the time. Honestly, I wish there was an easier answer, and I wish that I could tell you that in hindsight I didn't feel like I had wasted all this time making what seemed like the same mistakes, but the truth is all of it was necessary. You can never be wrong on the path that you take. Like I've mentioned before, there are many roads that lead to the same destination and part of the journey is learning to trust yourself and trust in life.

Trust that your unique path was necessary to get you to where you are now, and the things that are going to happen in the future are necessary for you to get to where you are going next. What is the point of regrets or wishing things could've been done differently? It only begets more of those feelings of shame and guilt you grew up with. I still have to remind myself of this, often!

If we had known certain things and learned certain things earlier, yeah, maybe the journey would be easier. I mean, that is exactly why I created *Lessons For My Daughters*. It is actually the reason why I'm writing this book. I'm hoping that you can piggyback on my experiences and that sharing my process will somehow lighten your load. The way others have done for me. Just trust that you are where you are meant to be right here, right now and there really are no such things as mistakes only lessons necessary for your growth.

It wouldn't be until almost twenty years after that first therapy appointment that I faced the real depth of my trauma again. I thought that knowing I didn't want to be like my parents was enough. I thought that if Nick and I loved each other, that would be enough to have a healthy marriage. I thought that if I loved my daughters enough, then that would be all I needed to be a great mother. And I wish love could be enough. Love is certainly the easy part. It's such a romanticized notion. However, when your earliest experiences of love are enmeshed with physical and emotional pain, it's pretty darn hard to discern what love really is. It's hard to discern what intimacy really is and what sex should be and what true pleasure is like. And it is certainly more difficult to give and receive love, to feel worthy of it.

I have felt a lot of regret in my life for bringing my daughters into the world before clearing up a lot of my pain. And when my oldest daughter, who like all of us has struggled and questioned life, said to me: "I didn't ask to be here," it really fucking hurt. But deep down I feel that even if she didn't *ask* to be here, not that she is consciously aware of at least, I like to think that we were most definitely supposed to be on this crazy ride called life together. And that maybe her presence was necessary to keep me looking forward to the future. I mean, she really was my reason to do better. My reason to live, to heal. Both of them have been. Now that's a huge burden for a child. I hope it didn't feel that way to her, but I know for certain that in many ways, like Nonna, she saved my life. She gave me purpose and meaning and reason to keep going. Both of my daughters did, and still do. My prayer is that one day they find that their journeys, their hardships, have led them to their purpose too.

As I mentioned earlier, I remember finding out that I was pregnant and I couldn't have been more excited. So excited that I was later accused of trying to entrap my boyfriend into marriage because I was too happy. For fuck's sake! What a stab at my happiness but it did not matter what others thought. And while trying to raise daughters surrounded by judgment that wasn't always easy but the truth was that my daughters taught me joy. My oldest taught me that what heals us does not always have to be painful but wildly wonderful. She represented an ease in my life that I had not known before.

And I have to say, in all of the dysfunction surrounding my life, the one thing I always knew I wanted was to be a mother. I oddly never dreamt of prince charming or white picket fences, just a person who would show me a love I had never known. Part of it was also my quest to want to do it better than my parents did. Perhaps these were all the wrong reasons. I mean I'm pretty sure they are. But when I look at my girls, I look at these two incredible beings of light. I see them as two powerful forces. I think to myself: "You are the only two things I ever did right in my life." So whatever led to your existence I know in my heart of hearts could never ever be a mistake. Not for one second.

There is no greater love than a love between a mother and her child. While I looked forward to having someone love me more than I had ever been loved, having the experience of being a mother made me understand my family even less. It made the grief and the pain that much more inexplicable because I didn't comprehend where their natural instincts of loving and protection had gone. And you know what? I'll never understand it. That is the one thing that I have had to make peace with because it is just a grief that never goes away. I hoped one day it would, but maybe it's not supposed to. Maybe for the first time in my life, I feel things so profoundly deep, and I see things for exactly what they are. Sometimes reality just sucks, and it absolutely was the truth for me.

It wasn't until the deep, spiritual, and sexual encounter that I was presented with facing myself once again. Remember Danny? The experience with him led me to try RET, and although that was a literal nightmare, I would revisit other forms of therapy time and again. I did acupuncture, massage, energy healing, and Reiki. I hired spiritual teachers, coaches, mentors, and enrolled in programs. I spent thousands upon thousands upon thousands of dollars, and you know what? It was all worth it. It was worth it to get to where I am today. At one point I was over $20,000 in debt, and I would do it all over again. There's no greater currency than health. It truly is the best investment and ripples out into all areas of your life. Looking back, I wish, like most things, that I hadn't waited so long. Doing so put me in a state of desperation. Don't let it come to that. If you know you had a traumatic past, take the steps to healing today, and trust the path life leads you when it comes to that healing.

I am not a mental health professional, but what makes me who I am is the fact that I came into this world as an innocent little girl faced with the ugliest of realities. I made it through the fire and came out a woman so strong, so in tune, and in many, many ways so unrecognizable to a former me just like the butterfly is to the caterpillar. People call me calm. They love my vibe, and I still get taken aback. This is very unlike the angry, cold, sarcastic, and insecure person I was.

I will say that energy work and physical touch have been the most profound modalities of healing for me personally as well as somatic experiencing therapy and incorporating movement into my daily practice. Remember, trauma lives in our cells. Our bodies remember every single thing that we have experienced, even when our logical mind cannot begin to fathom it and many times would not be able to handle it! As I have also mentioned, trauma is stored in the opposite part of the brain from language. Trauma lives in the right brain, the same as your creativity, like art and music, along with your emotions. Language is on the left, which is why it would make sense that other healing modalities might be more effective when you're in the process of healing and releasing.

For some of us our children are our drive to heal, for others we're still just too tired or overcome from the mistakes we've already made, whatever situation you're in. This is your reminder not to give up and just take one more step.

My girls, our children, are the *Super Generation*. They will fly further and faster than any generation before them.

Of all the titles life has given me, there has been no greater honor than to be a mother. To be relentlessly called Ma and Mom. I have loved every minute, every second. Even when it has been hard. They have been my reason to get up every morning and my motivation to fight through every single dark moment. I will never stop working hard, learning, growing, and being better for these two—my greatest gifts, my most incredible accomplishments. Although I have made them, they have made me. I will be eternally grateful to get to walk by their side in this crazy adventure we call life, and I pray every day for many, many more days and memories with each of them. I love these girls for infinity.

My Angel:

You know I've always wanted someone to love me the way you love me, and I got my wish. For a long time, it was still hard to actually take it all in and accept it. Although it was never your job to fill any of those deficiencies I felt within me, I'm so grateful for the gift that you are and have been in my life. You are the most perfect surprise I have ever received. Just to see how something that came from me could be as amazing as you is incredible. You're an incredible blend of strong, soft, vulnerable, emotional, serious, funny, intelligent, quiet, chatty, and all-around kick-ass. I always say I could never have dreamed of a more perfect kid. I didn't have hopes and dreams but you're better than anything I could have ever dreamt of, and for you I will always be grateful. You saved my life in many ways. Life has felt hard at times, and you have asked the question: what's the point? I promise that your presence in this world is so unequivocally meant to be. You are so loved and so needed, my Queen. Your light has changed my world and the world.

My Butterfly:

So perfect. So meant to be. Clear as the day when those two bright lines appeared, I knew you were the girl I have been waiting for. You are the perfect blend of sass and sweet. Never afraid to stick up for yourself or share what is in your mind or heart. I admire you so much. I love how much you know, all the incredible questions you ask. I still love it when you asked me why the trees lose their leaves when it's cold and they would be bare and that it would make more sense for them to shed their leaves in summer when it's hot. I love the way your mind works. The way you set an intention and it happens. I love even seeing that you really don't understand just how powerful you are, but that you grow into that power more and more each day. I love your passion and the way you shine so bright and I have always loved the way you have never cared what other people think. You are the epitome of dancing to the beat of your own drum. You inspire me. You light up my life, and I can't wait to see all the magic you will continue to create.

I hope that one day you both can understand just the way I see you. I am not sure. Maybe you'll have to be a mom to understand, but always remember: you are *everything* to me.

I also hope that you can understand more of why I made some of the choices I did. And while I am not perfect and have made many mistakes, I have always done my best to learn from them. So let that remind you that the mistakes are necessary and a gift in many ways but if any of those choices have ever hurt you, know that was never my intention. You are my love and my life and my reason for being and I know you will make incredible mothers one day (if you choose) and far surpass me in all ways and that truly is the point and don't ever even have to wonder because you already have.

Section 6

Super Generation

Support *Your* Super Generation

What can you do to model, teach, and support your *Super Generation*? First and foremost, heal yourself. This is the greatest gift you can give your children and, believe it or not, your ancestors as well. Imagine what we would not have passed on had we been guided to this work sooner? This is exactly why I do what I do. What would you tell your younger self? Start there.

Here are some tips for building connections: See her. Don't parent her through the lens of your trauma. Give her the freedom to lead and strengthen her butterfly wings—remember she is teaching you too.

Create and model healthy boundaries. This is so important for our daughters (and sons) too. This will increase their feelings of safety and security. Even though they may push those limits, they still need them and benefit from them. How would you rate yourself in this area? Do you find yourself negotiating or giving in? Are you being respectful and consistent as opposed to "barking orders" (those are the words my daughter has used to describe me at times) in the heat of the moment?

Love unconditionally. Loving unconditionally means more than saying, "I love you." It means loving them no matter what they do. Of course we do, but they may not always feel this way, and it may not always be easy for us to communicate it when they are acting or behaving in a way we might not like. Regardless, it is important to communicate our love to them in very specific ways. This may have seemed easier to do when they were babies. It can get harder when they start making their own decisions and we can confuse who our children ARE with what they are DOING. When we tie our love to their accomplishments, they do not feel good about themselves. They need to know that we accept who they are as the beautiful individuals they are and love them unconditionally. What do you think? Do you think your daughter feels accepted in her entirety by you?

Listen! Listening is so huge and not always easy! Our babies want to be seen, heard, and validated (all people do). When they feel listened to, they come away believing that what they had to say was valuable and that they contributed to the communication in a positive way. This makes them feel good about themselves. When your daughter is speaking, try not to criticize, give advice, or interject with ANYTHING. This can be difficult at times. This is something I continue to work on and have really struggled with. Our impulse to fix or make suggestions sometimes gets the better of us!

Think of the last time you spoke to your son or daughter. Were you really listening? Does he or she ever tell you that he or she feels you don't listen to or understand? Have you ever felt that way with someone? Do you find yourself just saying "okay" because you don't want them to know you didn't exactly hear it? What can you do to improve that?

Be affirming. How many times do our best intentions, for our children, get lost in translation? Deep inside you know they are capable of amazing things, but sometimes your exchanges can make you and them feel defeated. I know I have felt this way! Communicating that you believe they can handle a situation builds confidence. When you act like you don't believe they're capable, it sends the message that you expect that they will not succeed. This can seem crazy because that is not what we mean or intend to convey. We worry and want what is best for them; however, the message that comes across to our children can sometimes end up being different. How can you affirm your belief and confidence in your child even when you have genuine concerns? Conversely, how can you express your concerns without diminishing his or her confidence?

Let go. As parents we will have to let go many times over the course of the journey with our children. Some of the biggest things we need to let go of are our expectations. Oftentimes, our expectations can make our offspring feel like they are not good enough. Is there any one person in your life that has ever made you feel that way? What can you remind yourself of when you fear loosening the grip? Do you trust the foundation that you have laid out for them so far?

Take the time to journal about these ideas. Are there any areas you can make changes in?

What Would You Tell a Younger You?

Birthing a Super Generation has so much to do with giving our children everything we didn't have. There are so many things I wish I could have told the younger version of myself. Where can you find the golden nuggets in helping to raise the next generation with that information?

I would tell a younger me to heal and travel more and to do a lot more dating but really just to know yourself more before creating a life with someone else.

I would also tell her that she is loved and that she's beautiful and that "it wasn't your fault!" And from this new perspective you get to be the positive voice for your children now so they won't have as much to undo.

Also, it's easy to say "what if" or "I wish I . . ." that thing or the other, but they don't say hindsight is twenty-twenty for nothing. I would remind her there's a reason you didn't know better and remember to acknowledge and love yourself in all seasons and, for the love of God, give yourself *grace!* Modeling compassion and grace is a beautiful gift to give our kids and reminding them that failure truly is on the road to success.

Knowing Where to Start

With all the shit that was my life, it's no wonder interpersonal relationships were challenging. My experiences created a lot of brick walls that seemed to keep me in circles. However, I now know that healing is an ongoing journey. It's never ending.

There's always more to learn, to discover, until life here is done. It can be exhausting but at the same time that is why we are here to continue to elevate.

Despite this knowing, sometimes it can feel so overwhelming and we don't know where to start. Well, where in your life is there friction or pain? That is where the work begins and even if it seems like there are so many, start with one. But nowadays I try not to look at it as healing anymore. Like I said, the word implies you are sick or unwell, which although it may seem true, it is not at the deepest level. The unchanging part of you can never be irrevocably altered. To me it's more of an unbecoming or coming back home to yourself.

The wound is where the light enters and, God, it can be excruciating. The triggers, the unraveling, the panic, the feeling of "you must be fucking crazy." That uneasiness in your body or the numbness, or the disconnectedness? Even so, I promise you, looking at it is worth it.

Remember, all magic happens in the dark. Your body went through trauma; therefore, your body is necessary for healing. So much of what we consider "mental illness" is the fact that all of these experiences and the emotions tied to them remain unprocessed and stuck. Your body is a safe place and will always tell you what she needs. Allow it to flow through and release without the attachment of your mind. It starts with you.

You are a change agent. You are responsible for passing that baton. You are the epitome of a butterfly's journey and now you know it's not all about YOU! Shedding those layers is also about those who came before us as well as the legacy we are leaving behind. Imagine that this moment, this journey is just a small speck in the grander, greater scheme of things that is utterly incomprehensible currently. It is out of focus and that is where the trust comes in. Believe that you are an integral piece of the whole, and that one piece is enormously powerful in itself because the whole could not exist without YOU. If you are here, you have purpose. If you take anything from all of this, remember that key thing.

Get quiet, listen. The next step is always there. Whatever you have been presented with, you can get through it. Not only will you get through it, but you will also be transformed—and you will be better, deeper, stronger, more resilient, wiser, and more connected to your power.

Can you allow yourself to truly soak that in?

Own Your Power

Life is a beautiful and intricate web. You can't change one thing without affecting another. Everything is so intertwined. One event leads to another until in the end, you end up with something beautiful: your life, your story. But we shouldn't wait until the end to appreciate the tapestry and enjoy every blend, every snag, every imperfection.

Honor your talent, acknowledge its beauty, and every once in a while, take a step back to enjoy the art, the magic you've created so far. Be in this *now* moment. The only one that truly exists.

There will always be ebbs and flows, and that is all there to teach you where the triggers remain. Part of it is, well . . . just life. Loss, grief, heartache. You can now feel the highs more deeply but along with that you feel the lows more completely. You won't get lost there or sucked in like quicksand. You'll feel more like a leader in your own life and at large (if you are so called to). You'll live life with intention; knowing full well you are the director of the show, orchestrating with the divine. You'll be more open to love, to pleasure. You'll see things more clearly. That path before you. You'll feel more connected to your purpose. You will once and for all own your power!

The more I untangled myself, the more I learned. And let's be clear, I am still on that journey, and as long as I am alive, I will be; as long as we are here, there are still beautiful lessons to learn. But the thing that surprised me the most was the clarity. The feeling in control and organized. The diminishing doubt. I know that my dreams are literally unfolding before me. I don't worry about how anymore. I feel so much more intentional with every little aspect of my life. How I spend and earn money. Where I put my attention. I'm clearer on the kind of leader, lover, teacher, friend, nurturer, author, mother, sister, daughter, and wife I want to be. It feels like a lot, but it's also simpler as well.

Tips for Your Journey

- Trust the process—beginnings and endings are natural and okay!
- Forget all stories of how ANYTHING should be, look, or feel.
- Let go of needing to control and be in the flow. Detachment works.
- Trust yourself—following that inner knowing but be open to what you don't know.
- Let go of the idea of *needing to know*, because ultimately isn't that the beauty of life?
- Don't be afraid of not knowing. Not knowing when it will be our last day or how any of it will turn out.

That's the part that makes it more precious. That fact is what should make you feel grateful for every fucking second, minute, hour!

- Be here now.

And don't forget: your flight, your story, your journey is not over. You have more important work to do. Remember that you are enough. You will continue to make mistakes and that's okay—it's all part of the learning. And don't forget to celebrate yourself. You are worth celebrating and every little milestone along the way! And with each step, know that you are doing it. You are ending generational trauma!

Embrace what MADE you.

You are a total badass. You have always been on the right path.

Honor where you have been and get crystal clear on your knowing, the knowing of who YOU are and where the fuck you are going.

You are invincible and are interconnected to the miracles that exist in every moment. YOU ARE THAT INDESCRIBABLE MIRACLE.

Stay away from anyone or anything that may make you feel otherwise.

We are not all the same. People like us are not just born; we are made.

I have been to the depths of hell. Some may call it an initiation, others a nightmare—regardless of how you see it, there's a strength that comes from survival, a strength that cannot come any other way. And while it may have sucked to have been burned to get where you are, I will be damned if I let my experiences or yours be in vain.

My life is not my own. None of ours are. My job is to pull people forward with the knowledge I have been gifted with. Be on this journey with me.

The world needs you to own your power today.

And I have had to let go of my conditioning to realize just how wonderful my world is. There comes a time when you sink into the beauty of the moment. Life is rarely how you plan it. Mine is certainly not in any way I imagined. In my high school yearbook, there was a question: "Where do you want to be in ten years?" I had one simple response: "Happy." Well, it's been over twenty years, and I've come to realize that happiness is not the goal. You'll never feel happy every day, but underneath it you can feel content and at peace no matter what is happening externally. To a certain extent, you really do have to let go of the life you planned in order to live the life meant for you. Celebrate all that is and I celebrate you and I thank you for being a part of this journey with me no matter how big or how small.

Section 7

Final Thoughts

Inner Child Healing/Integration

The child within you is still alive and well. Acknowledge her, honor her, and know that you very much can give her the things she needed then, now. Your ability to heal her, to validate her is real and powerful and transformational. This work not only heals you and those who come after you, but that it also affects those who came before you. Time is not linear, and your intentions can move mountains, trust me.

Safety Comes from Within

Another huge lesson I learned was that my safety was in my hands now. Safety is not something you find outside of yourself. I used to think the idea of safety came from an outside source.

When you're a kid, it does. It's a feeling you get from your parents. Through their words, actions, and the physical expressions of meeting your basic needs. Without that, it makes navigating life moving forward more difficult because you constantly feel ungrounded, on high alert, and have an overall feeling of being unsafe. If you didn't have it growing up, it is normal to feel that way now.

I felt that way, but I wasn't conscious of it. I felt abandoned, discarded—a feeling of not being worth anything. Not being worth protecting, believing, or loving. So I believed that to be my truth. Even though externally I may have come off confident, energy is everything, so over time I would create more experiences that would mirror this truth I had about myself.

I felt like I needed to chase love. That I had to find my worth outside of myself. That something was out there always just beyond my reach. But I'm learning to be still now. Not to chase. To go inside. To blossom into the most beautiful flower and allow. Allow all of life's joys, pleasures, lessons, and experiences to wash over me—like a beautiful gift, always deepening who I am, never taking away from me.

Never giving away a piece of myself. No longer changing or contorting to receive but simply allowing, being, remembering that the simple act of being alive is representative of a miracle that's been activated.

And being a part of that miracle, a real-life expression of magic—that fact alone means that I am deserving. I am worthy. I am all that is good and all that is good surrounds me. And although I may not have that physical presence in the form of parents to make me feel safe, I have learned and felt my connection to all that is, which supports me in the biggest way possible. The Earth is my home, and she is the ultimate Mother. Being grounded to her is a way for me to remember there is always a home to return to. If anytime I feel unstable or unsure, I can go to her and connect to her and remember who I am once again.

The Power of Routines

I had no choice but to find homeostasis, and one of the ways to do that was within a routine. And I didn't think about it—it just happened. That's how I know that knowing what you need is an intuitive thing. Doing this really helped me to recalibrate my nervous system to baseline. Growing up surrounded by trauma, I often felt chaos in my mind. So much of what shows up outside of you is a reflection of what's going on inside you. Are things chaotic, messy, disorganized? Chances are that's the state of your internal landscape as well.

As a child raised in disorder you would think I'd crave a predictable routine. I was just the opposite—routines felt stifling and controlling to me. I always hated them, but subconsciously I think I loved them too. I'm one hundred percent a "go with the flow" kind of gal with a side of trying to control things out of my control (working on it). Paradoxical I know.

When you find a routine that works for you, it no longer feels like a chore; it's rather like something you intentionally chose, something that grounds you into your sense of safety and well being. If it doesn't—change it until it does. One day my daughter told me that it was impossible to remember all the rules she had to follow to make sure she didn't get injured from jumping on the trampoline that she loves so much. I said: "You never forget to brush your teeth or your hair, right? That's a routine. Just add a next step to the things you do already."

The way you start your day and end your day are so important. I like to think of it as a positive sandwich!

Morning routines set the tone for everything else you have going on, and a nighttime routine helps you go into your rest and replenish with less on your mind, which will in turn affect the next day too.

Here are some things I do. This may seem like a long list but it doesn't require much time.

Step 1. Gratitude. As soon as I open my eyes, I pause and feel into my body. Then I simply say thank you. If you really allow this feeling, you'll realize the magnitude and gift of simply waking up another day.

Step 2. Meditation. Some people say prayer is talking to God (or whatever you identify with) and meditation is listening to God. Take 1–3 minutes to just observe your thoughts without judgment and watch them float away without attachment. This gives you insight into what's weighing on your mind, and it is also a wonderful way to let all that go. Think of the thoughts as bubbles and just watch them pop, pop, pop as they go by. When you do this, oftentimes it leaves space for the answers to your life's questions. Yes, you have more access to that information than you think!

Step 3. Prayer. Here's where I set intentions for what I'm creating for my life and the world. Mostly asking to be a clear vehicle to do the work I am meant to do here and being thankful for everything that already is. There's a great practice where you make two to-do lists. One column has the things you're personally working on, and the second is your column to "give to

God." That is where you learn to trust that the things we can't humanly wrap our brain around in terms of "how am I gonna make this happen"—will find a way. I also ask for safety and protection for myself and my loved ones and always throw in some more gratitude.

Here's a sample prayer:

Dear God the father, blessed Mother, all that is holy and all knowing. Thank you for another day. Thank you for all of our gifts. Please allow to peacefully unfold what is in the best interest of all of us and please keep us safe in mind, body, soul, and spirit— myself, my beloved, my girls. Help us to create the space for allowing miracles into our lives and for trusting. Work through us to bring about positive change here. Please keep us safe, healthy, and feeling good. Amen.

Step 4. Hydrate. What we consume internally also makes a big impact on our productivity, clarity, mood, and inner peace. I always start the day with a tall glass of room temperature water and lemon. Lime works well too. The room temperature part is important as water that is too cold will shock your warm system. This also helps to delay breakfast, which for me is usually fruit. I won't have a cooked meal (usually eggs) until at least four hours after I wake up. Then I will take some vitamins and minerals for healthy brain function. Some people feel it is important to break the fast earlier, but again always make changes based on what feels right to you.

Step 5. Journal. Writing is another great way to get out what may be stuck ruminating inside you. A lot of times, social media becomes a place of journaling for me since I love sharing my thoughts and process in an attempt to help or inspire someone else. However, it's good to do a free write with no actual intention behind it. Think of it as sort of a mind dump, just writing everything that comes into your stream of consciousness. What comes out can really surprise you! Again, no judgment, it's important not to take all of our thoughts as actual facts.

After the mind dump, you can write gratitudes for the present, you can write gratitudes for the things that are to come and you can also just write out what you envision for your life. Take some time every day to daydream about the life you are creating.

Step 6. Movement. Moving your body is so important to incorporate into your everyday life, especially if our work routines are largely sedentary or we are working from home or at a computer all day. Stretch, take a walk, dance, go for a bike ride, hula hoop, do any sort of workout that feels good to you. Whatever it is that gets the blood and endorphins flowing. It also feels so good to sweat because this is a great way to detox. I personally love to start the day with yoga. It feels flowy and not super strenuous, but as you increase your strength and stamina, you can choose to challenge yourself. Set an intention for your day with whatever you choose to do. Put on some relaxing and restorative music such as 528Hz music, which can easily be searched on any platform.

Step 7. Tidy. I'm personally a morning person. I prefer to straighten up in the morning because having a clean and organized space helps clear my mind, and it's helpful to have a clean space before tackling work for the day. See what works for you. If this is an area that is difficult for you, understand that it's okay to only do a little bit every day. Reduce the clutter around you, and you will see a difference in how your day moves forward. As a side note, the more you transform from the inside out, the more you will see that reflected in the space around you.

A nighttime routine is just as important. You want to create a practice where you're not taking the entire day into your sleep and inevitably into the next day.

Step 1. Tidy. Take some time to put away anything that's out of place. This doesn't have to be *everything*, but like we did in the morning, start with a few items. If this feels overwhelming, allowing yourself the grace and leaving it for the next day is okay too.

Step 2. Make a To-Do List. Organize for yourself what you have planned the next day. I personally love a paper calendar/organizer. I try to put in all the events I remember for the upcoming month and then add lists as I go.

Step 3. Cleanse. Cleanse your body and or your energy or both. Take a nice bath or shower, or do a mind dump or a movement practice. See this as a way to clear your mind, body, and spirit. Set the intention that you are releasing the day's troubles so you don't have to carry them into the next day.

Step 4. Tea. Drink something calming like chamomile. This tea helps me to relax. Hot water also helps to digest. See what works for you.

Step 5. Movement. Incorporate some movement if you didn't do so already. You can do some stretching. I really love yoga at the end of the day as well. Search "Yoga with Adriene" or "Yoga with Kassandra." Those are my two favorites. They both have short routines available. The quick five-minute routines felt like such a life saver for me when I had zero energy for anything more.

Step 6. Prayer/Gratitudes. Like the morning, count your blessings.

Here's a sample prayer:

Dear God the father, blessed Mother, all that is holy and all knowing. Thank you for another day and all the gifts you have given us. Please bless our lives and our spirits. Keep our minds clear, our hearts open, and our bodies healthy. Keep us safe from harm. Allow us to fulfill our life's purpose. Please strengthen our connection and love to each other and to the divine.

May we sleep peacefully and soundly. Bless our home and all who enter. Keep us free from negativity. Bless our animals and our families and friends. Bless our neighborhood, community, country, and planet. All my love and gratitude. Amen.

Step 7. Meditation. Empty your mind before going to sleep. Take 1–3 minutes to just observe your thoughts without judgment and watch them float away without attachment.

How does that sound and feel? Feel free to change the order, and omit or add whatever you would like. If it feels overwhelming, start with one or two. Find what feels truly nourishing to your body and soul.

Affirmations

Affirmations have been a very powerful tool for me. There was a time I had to write myself notes everywhere to remind myself of my worth. I recorded myself saying positive things about myself and I would listen to it on repeat. Some people say affirmations don't work because in a way it feels like you're lying to yourself. I feel like it does. And the way to fix the fibbing part is to modify the statement until it is better than what you believe but still feels true. For example I once was working with my somatic therapist and working through the grief I felt over failing at marriage and the statement she had me say was that my daughters were happy. It immediately felt like a lie because I knew my choices inevitably affected them and sometimes in a negative way. Divorce is ultimately a trauma. I changed the statement to my daughters are loved. And from there I felt my heart expand because yes they are so, so deeply loved. So modify what you need to in order to believe it and then grow from there.

Finding Your Way Home

While there is no cookie cutter recipe and every journey is unique, I want to share with you some of the other things that I have been led to over the years.

First, it is important to remember that not all practitioners are created equal. There are people who are good and bad in what they do in every profession, and there will be modalities that mesh well with you and others that don't. You'll learn to feel what's best for you. As I have shared, I am not a mental health professional by any means, but by the same token I feel experience is the best teacher. If I am honest with myself, I have reaped the most rewards from those who followed their innate ability to heal and shared that with the world. They didn't necessarily have "mental health" degrees, and some of the most amazing people I know combine several different modalities into one and make their own magic. As always, trust yourself.

In my journey to coming home to myself, I tried many different things. I was desperate to feel whole, and the more I connected with my spiritual side, the greater my world and awareness opened up around me. It helped me see all the wonderful ways to rediscover myself, to have a new relationship with the self. So much of it pointed me back to myself as the source of my own healing. And while we call the journey healing, it may feel implied that you're shattered in some way. I just want to remind you that you are never irreparably broken. And when I say come home to myself, I mean feeling connected to myself, to my purpose, not feeling lost like I am a result of circumstance, but rather living life with intention. Getting rid of that nagging feeling that something is missing. Feeling energized about the path I am on and feeling in flow.

Although ALL the work I did (and all the help I received from others on my journey) led me to where I am today, some work stands out more than others.

As I became older and wiser, I really focused so much on the mind, body, and soul connection. There really is no separation, and you can't have total wellness when any of these areas is out of alignment. I know that your state of physical health absolutely one hundred percent affects your emotional health. I was on a quest to find balance within myself.

At the most difficult point in my journey, I could hardly eat. I was using phone apps to count calories to make sure I was getting enough food intake. By this time, I was thankfully tapped into a huge network of holistic minded people and someone mentioned functional medicine. Functional medicine takes a whole body approach to healing and they focus on food and nutrition. I sought out a functional medicine practitioner. They take an unbelievable amount of bloodwork to test things down to very minute functions. Things that traditional doctors overlook. I thought I would die from the lab work alone! Although I'm not sure how much the functional medicine piece really helped, it was through it that I met Julianna. Sessions with her came with the whole healing package I purchased. She did acupuncture, craniosacral therapy, and Reiki. Although I had experienced two out of the three of these modalities before, she had a magic all her own as she combined all three, which is why it's the person who matters so much more than the title. No matter how bad I was feeling, when I got there, I knew I'd feel more balanced when I left. She explained how since my anxiety was in my thoughts, it was almost as if I was floating away through my head. She just kept telling me I needed to work on being more grounded. I would go on to hear this again and again.

Energy work is completely mind blowing. I knew that from past experiences, but the way it was making a difference now was so much more prominent. I called every healing person I knew for recommendations. An old friend Ruth returned to my sphere, and she did Emotion Code and Body Code with me. These both help to release trapped emotions in your body, energetically as well as to help find the root causes of any disease in body and spirit. So much suffering is caused by unprocessed and trapped emotions. Since some of them were buried so deep, I sought out all the help I could get.

I also sought out acupuncture. This is also something I had tried before for a previous unrelated (or not) issue. I am not sure how I found Caitlin, but she was instrumental in my healing. She really sat and listened. She had so much knowledge in various protocols. I will never forget after one session that was focused on me using my voice to speak my truth—I literally began singing out of nowhere for hours following the session—a "song from my heart." I sang and I cried all this trapped pain inside. If I had not personally experienced it, I honestly would never believe it.

Not soon after I worked with Ruth and Caitlin, I met Cara. She is a Nambudripad Allergy Elimination Technique or NAET practitioner. We did emotional release with NAET as well and then moved on to incorporating Emotion Code and Body Code too. Sessions with her began in person. Sometimes

I needed to be there two times a week. I required so much assistance in feeling grounded and safe, but deep down I knew the end goal was to do much of it for myself. But as someone who never felt like I had much support, I think this worked in healing me on various levels. To trust people with this level of pain and vulnerability and feel safe after all I had been through with family and professionals alike—it was big for me.

Remember I said life is always giving you signs? Trust that the next step will always be revealed to you. I remember commenting on something on either mine or someone else's Facebook post. I am not sure I even remember who the person is anymore and if I actually knew her but she mentioned Somatic Therapy, which was mentioned to me years prior to this. She asked if I wanted to be connected to someone who made a big difference in her life, and I said yes. This woman gave me Alycia's information, and the work I did with her became the most powerful and transformative to date.

Releasing through movement? It's like my body always knew this, but here I was incorporating it into my journey to feeling whole with intention. It was the most beautiful, moving, and incredibly profound experience. Although I did so much work, my time with Alycia was where I felt I was getting the most concrete results. Like permanent shifts back to me. I could feel the change from survival to thriving. In fact, after any one of these forms of realignment I could feel physical weight lift from me, my digestion flowing. I felt clearer in my thoughts, less angry, more loving, more forgiving. It is completely life altering.

In my healing network, I was also introduced to homeopathy. Again, something I used religiously when my kids were sick, but I had no idea that it could help with trauma.

Jonathan, another beautiful healer, took a thorough inventory of where I was, what I had been through, what I was feeling. And what was more incredible was that he gifted his sessions to me because he was just beginning his journey as a homeopathic practitioner. He narrowed down a remedy. It cost me only a few dollars, and I also saw dramatic shifts in my life.

It was amazing. What I find even more incredible is that there are truly so many roads you can take. There is so much available to us. We know so much more now about the mind, body, spirit connection. It's a beautiful dance. Everything is so connected. Spinal alignment, nutrition, posture, breathing, muscular tension—you name it. You are a beautiful web of magnificent things working together to bring you to a place of homeostasis. Be in cooperation. Sure, our lives, our stories, our experiences can have a way of knocking us so far off center that we may not see a way back, but it is possible. All you have to do is start somewhere and you will have more options. And these forms of self-care are what we need in our lives—even when things seem great. I continue to see many of these practitioners today.

Grieving and Forgiveness

On my path, there were certain things I needed to figure out for myself. One of those things was understanding grief. I always thought healing meant not being hurt by the past any longer. I thought that one day this just would not be my story. What actually happens is how you tell your story. This does not mean that the loss is no longer there. That would be like telling someone whose loved one has passed that one day you'll no longer feel that way. Grief and loss do not work that way.

I will, in some way shape or form, always feel the loss of not having two parents who knew how to love me and keep me safe. I will feel sad that as much as I wanted to get it right for my own kids, I didn't. But I don't allow myself to live there. I don't stay in that place, but I want this to serve as a reminder that it's okay to grieve what could have been.

Allowing yourself to feel grief is a big part of the journey. It's a huge part of letting the heaviness of the past go. When we are numb for a long time, we want to keep going without having to feel. But your body is carrying the weight of it even if you are not aware of it. It is necessary to grieve for our little selves who were dealt a rough hand. Our parents' little selves were undoubtedly dealt their own raw deal. Go back as far as you can imagine to each generation before that. In this way, we see how the trauma gets passed down. Some want to acknowledge it, others don't, but when we step back and see the patterns as a whole, it's evident.

It is also okay for you to separate yourself from unhealthy people. Family is one thing when you're in a place of love, safety, and care, but when you're talking about people who are bad for you, bad in the way you can feel it—trust me, this is not family. You will find family elsewhere, a family of your own choosing. It is always better to be alone than in the wrong company, as hard as that may be. I have found family to equate to love and safety and not something that requires a biological connection.

I also hear a lot about forgiveness—the idea that you need to forgive others in order to heal. I, for one, find some things unforgivable, especially when those who have done the hurting refuse to acknowledge the impact of that on you. To me, that does not warrant forgiveness. And this idea that forgiveness is for you and not them? I can heal without forgiving deplorable actions. I am proof of that. The only forgiveness I have to truly give is to myself and that has not been easy. Forgive yourself for not knowing, for trusting, for not saying anything, and for making decisions based on that pain. Release yourself from that burden. And just because you don't forgive what others have done doesn't mean you hold on to hate or resentment, but when forgiveness just doesn't feel justified in certain situations, know that is okay.

Finale

Although writing has always been very healing for me, on some level I spent a lot of my life in fear of it. In high school, I was forced to keep a journal by my English teacher. Although I often hinted at the reality of my life, I was always vague. Mrs. Rosenberg always asked me to expand on my ideas, but I never could. I felt like writing down the story of my life would make it painfully real and irrevocably true. I spent thirty-eight years in many ways avoiding the horror that was my life, both consciously and subconsciously, until the facade began to crumble and I was forced to face it. I kept making bad choices, despite what I was being shown until I sank into a dark abyss. I was literally unable to walk from my bed to the kitchen, feeling like I didn't have enough air in my lungs to utter one more word. My spiritual teacher Iris told me when I came through it, I'd be able to tell my story. Although I could not see beyond the frightening place I was in, I knew she was right. I knew I was meant to write it, and although it has taken quite a few stops and starts, it is finally here and like the butterfly—it has been quite the transformational experience. I am not the same person I was when I began.

Life is a continuum and I am a bridge between those who came before me, to those who have come through me, to those who will come after me, and a beautiful web encompassing all those who have entered and exited my life throughout the years. Our lives are not meant only for ourselves. We are here to continue the work of our ancestors. Or, in many cases, to right their wrongs and to pass the baton to our children and eventually our children's children and so on. Time is neither linear nor finite, and many of us have yet to truly discover the depths of our reach.

I am just one person, but I am also a vehicle for spirit to express itself and live through me to do something great with my life. We all are here for that very reason, and it doesn't have to look like a long list of grandiose accomplishments but more of a returning to and a remembering of who we are.

Some may say the only purpose in life is the purpose you give it. As humans we attach meaning to so many things, sometimes through the lens of our ego. But there are those moments that logic simply cannot explain. The miracles that seem otherwise unbelievable, but I am certain magic exists every day. I hope I have helped you tune into seeing the world through a new perspective.

You are safe now. It wasn't your fault. You're okay, and it is okay to feel safe, as it is okay to feel joy. It is okay to forgive yourself now and know that you are protected and guided. It is time to believe that you are ready to align your life to peace, to pleasure, and to finally give yourself grace. Grace for where you have been, and grace on the road to the next chapter. You are ready to receive life's gifts, to fully embody your humanness and no longer be afraid of it. You are ready for a deeper sense of trust in yourself and life free of family trauma.

Envision yourself grounded in your ability to remain centered and present even when it is uncomfortable. Of course, there will always be aspects of life out of your control. However, how you respond is entirely up to you.

What is the most beautiful version of your life you can imagine? Live it and claim it. You deserve it. Remember that wellness and peace are your birthright. And if you feel lost, don't be afraid to reach out for support. Don't ask people for directions to places they have never been to. Surround yourself with those who have achieved what you are aspiring to.

Although it is this part of ourselves where we have experienced the greatest pain that keeps us from living to the fullest, it is also the very place inside us where we must go for the key to healing. It is also where we are called to have the most compassion for ourselves.

Celebrate yourself in all your humanness. Even when you mess up. Know your beauty, your power, your brilliance and use that to fuel what you desire. You can write a new story. Nurture your own lost child. Feel the rage of never being seen or heard and of being told what to think and what to do. Feel the rage of living behind a lie.

But be easy on yourself. You are learning a new way of being. Know how important you are, you are valued, needed, and so loved. And the most important thing, don't be afraid of total deconstruction. As the butterfly teaches us, it is essential to birth anew.

I too have to remind myself of all of these things, and I am always learning. As chapters closed and new ones began, I was called to dive deeper into many of these lessons. My body is always speaking to me and there have been times where I have been brought to my knees because I went on ignoring her for a little too long. Embodying ourselves and this life completely is not easy, but it makes our time here so much deeper, richer, and rewarding. When we are fully here, we can make the most of our gifts and ensure the birth of the next Super Generation and the one after that. It is an honor to be on this butterfly journey with you.

I am excited to expand my work as a human, as a Wife, Mother, Reiki Master, Healer, Teacher, Author, Coach, and to discover new gifts to share and paths along the way I did not know existed. And I am wishing you the same for you.

Resources

Healer Directory

Name	Profession	Contact
Nicole Anastas Higgins	Massage and Yoga Therapy	978-801-1008
Daniela Barnett	RN, Massage Therapist, Reiki Master	
Christina Barr	Acupuncturist	PrismAcu.com
Caitlin Bree	Acupuncturist	Acupuncture.com
Cara DiCicco-Sandre	Certified NAET Practitioner	BalanceYourEnergy.health
Adam Hakim	Certified Craniosacral Therapist	HakimHealthcare.com
Jonathan Kavner	Homeopath	LongIslandHomeopath.com
Gina LaVerde	Medical Intuitive	Gina@BlissedLife.com
Kate MacKinnon	Certified Feng Shui Practitioner	Kate-MacKinnon.com
Donna McGrath	Energy Master/ Medical Medium	DonnaMcGrath.com
Claudia Phillips	Dating and Marriage Mentor	ecstaticallyeverafter.com
Tina Ryan	Massage Therapist	631-807-4451

Name	Profession	Contact
Alycia Scott Zollinger	Somatic Healing Facilitator	AlyciaZollinger.com
Joshua Siegel	Chiropractor	CafeofLifeLongIsland.com
Dr. Alan Sherr	Chiropractor	NorthportWellnessCenter.com
Staci Snair	Energy Healer, Medium, Reiki Master	StaciSnair.com
Dr. Jess Tregle, Msc.D	Energy Healer	DrJessTregle.com

Book Recommendations

Title	Author
Stolen Tomorrows	Steven Levenkron
Peace from Broken Pieces	Iyanla Vanzant
Welcome to Your Crisis	Laura Day
The Power of Now	Eckhart Tolle

Instagram

Name	Instagram Handle
Nate Postlethwait	@nate_postlethwait
Dr. Nicole LePera	@the.holistic.psychologist
Erika Polsinelli	@inkale.exkale

Free Resources

The beach, dancing, meditation, screaming, crying, yoga, long baths, anything that feels good to you that does not harm anyone else. You are amazing and wise and intuitive.

Acknowledgments

An enormous thank you to every single person who has made this dream of a book into a reality. To the family and friends who encouraged me to tell my story and speak my truth. To my book coach, Heather, and all the beautiful authors in my cohort. To Azul (which so fittingly means blue) and Steve, who cultivated such a safe and inviting space to let these butterfly wings fly. To Kim for her support and endless patience, and to all the editors and contributors: Lauren, Justin, Melissa, and Valene. A big acknowledgment to Ann, who helped to develop this grand butterfly vision, and to Kaitlin, for executing an incredible cover and interior design. From the bottom of my heart, thank you.

About the Author

Carmin Caterina is a former school-based, NYC speech language pathologist who turned her love of helping others find their voice into something deeper.

Using the tools that helped her get through a violent and traumatic life, she helps women transform into the best versions of themselves not only for themselves but also for their own children.

Because she didn't have a lot of support or direction growing up, Carmin had to gauge what healthy behavior looked like between what she watched on television and what she saw modeled in her friends' homes. She always had a love and desire to work with children and protect them, so she focused her career on education and healthcare—specifically speech language pathology—to help others find their voice in a very literal way.

This career took on greater meaning when she created a curriculum specifically to empower young girls. This is how her organization, Lessons For My Daughters, was born and from there her Girl Powered and Project Happiness curriculums.

As she has expanded as a healer and coach, Carmin's services became more and more sought-after by women for themselves. This inspired her to document her own story in this book and simultaneously led her to create her signature program: *Embodiment: 45 days to Peace + Pleasure + Grace*, a transformational journey for women that encompasses many of the tools she used in her own healing journey.

Carmin is a mother, teacher, author, coach, speaker, and Reiki Master. She lives in her dream home in Long Beach, New York, with her two daughters and cat Fudge. Her love of the beach has inspired her to create seashell art in her spare time.

I would appreciate your feedback on what chapters helped you most and what you would like to see in future books.

If you enjoyed this book and found it helpful, please leave a review on Amazon.

Visit me at

CARMINCATERINA.COM

where you can sign up for email updates.

Thank you!